THE GREATEST OFFER

THE GREATEST OFFER

Reconsidering the Christian Faith in Light of Contemporary Evidence

Dr. James Saxon

Carpenter's Son Publishing

The Greatest Offer: Reconsidering the Christian Faith
in Light of Contemporary Evidence

Published by Carpenter's Son Publishing, Franklin, Tennessee
www.christianbookservices.com

Edited by Bob Irvin

Cover and Interior Layout Design by Suzanne Lawing

ISBN: 978-1-956370-98-0 (print)

Printed in the United States of America

DEDICATION

I dedicate this book to all my high school friends and classmates who kept the God-question before me when I was far from him in my teenage years. There are too many names to mention, but you know who you are, and most importantly, the Lord knows the service you rendered to his name and to my soul by not being ashamed of the true way to God in our younger years!

CONTENTS

ACKNOWLEDGMENTS

I would like to thank The Church of The Apostles in Atlanta, Georgia for the opportunity to serve as Director of Evangelism for the last two decades. During that time the material covered in this book was assembled in the form of a course and now into this book.

My special thanks to the Founding Rector, Dr. Michael Youssef, for putting me in the "point man" role of reaching souls when it was decided that the church needed to intensify its efforts in this area in 2005.

A special thanks to the team of volunteers at Apostles who gave up many a Saturday morning and weeknight to serve as table leaders for the Christianity Examined course while it was being taught at the church, since 2012, the year we launched the effort. These especially include Susan White, Mark Kraft, and Ken Fuller, but there are many others.

Through my pastoral years I have enjoyed many effective administrative assistants, and the one who helped me develop this course from the beginning, Jan Blakeslee, has been a true partner in this effort. She understood the creative energy that was involved and confirmed the value of the course by bringing family members and friends to it, some of whom became followers of Jesus as a result.

My thanks to my wife and helper, Cindy, who was the first person to come to the Lord in the church I planted in Tampa, Florida in 1979. She has sacrificed much time with her husband while I was involved in caring for souls throughout our forty-three years of marriage. Her impact on her own family for the Lord proved to me long ago that, between the two of us, she really is much better at introducing people to the Lord than I am.

Finally, thanks to my two daughters, Natalie and Adrienne; my son-in-law, Chris; my grandson, Harrison; and my granddaughter, Savannah, for the daily joy they all bring to my life in between all the things God has called me to do.

FOREWORD

Back in the 1970s, I heard an Englishman speak on evangelism; he called it "the Cinderella of the church." People know all about it, they acknowledge it, and they may want to do something about it. But, in the end, they ignore it and pretend it is not a very significant part of God's household.

We often say that the last words of the dearly departed are the most important, but somehow, we do not apply this maxim to the last words of Jesus before He departed our Earth to go back to His Heaven.

At the end of every one of the four Gospels and in the beginning of the book of Acts, Jesus repeatedly told His disciples that they must be witnesses, make disciples, be on a mission, and think of themselves as "sent" just as much as He was sent by the Father.

Sadly, even among our mega churches, leaders will implement any and every genre of program to attract new people—except for the only one that Jesus commissioned us to bring into being.

Terms like "soul winning" and "reaching the lost" are considered passé to modern-day evangelicals, yet these intentional activities are the actual signs of spiritual life and vitality.

For more than four decades, James Saxon has been intentional in obeying our Lord's great commission. From his earliest years in ministry when he birthed a church in Florida to his more than two decades at The Church of the Apostles in Atlanta, he has intentionally reached out with love to many.

His experience is rich with practical examples of hours spent talking with and listening to those who either did not know, or had a very vague notion of, who Jesus is. Then he provided them with opportunities and a place where they grew in Christ. James was so effective in his mission that he led a young woman to Christ who later became his wife.

The book you have in your hands (or on the screen before you) is the distillation of James's four decades of genuinely and intensely investing in the talks I mentioned above. You will be blessed to read about the fruit of these encounters.

I am certain that whether you are a lay leader or an ordained minister, you will be blessed, encouraged, and motivated when you read *The Greatest Offer.* This is not just a great offer to whoever might listen, it is "the greatest offer" we can present to a desperately confused generation.

Michael Youssef, PhD
Atlanta, Georgia
June 2025

AUTHOR'S NOTE: HOW THIS BOOK CAME TO BE

This book represents hundreds of hours spent in God-conversations with people across the last forty-five years of pastoral ministry. Though I do not have the gift of evangelism, I think it is fair to say that I am an evangelistic pastor. I have seen many people enter a personal relationship with God through Jesus, and my life has become defined by the fact that there is no joy equal to the joy of seeing a person come to a peaceful resting place in their relationship with God. Here is how I became fully absorbed in helping people discover the true way to God.

Soon after I joined the staff of The Church of The Apostles in Atlanta, Georgia, in the fall of 2000, I was asked by one of our church members, "If a person walked into our church and wanted to know how to have a personal relationship with God, where would they go?" Initially, I was caught off guard by the question and was even more stunned by my lack of an answer! We didn't have a class or a course to send people to who wanted help in understanding how to connect with God. I had no answer to his question that, honestly, caught me completely flatfooted.

A few years later, as Apostles entered a rapid growth phase after its marvelously beautiful sanctuary opened, I became concerned that the church was not fulfilling its mission of reaching out to people in need of God. After I had done a thousand or so new member interviews, I concluded that the vast majority of people entering the fellowship of our church had a viable faith already in place *before* they began attending Apostles. So, a bit naively, I approached the rector (senior pastor) and informed him of my uneasy discovery, and he encouraged me to try to find a qualified person who could fill that staff gap. I was unsuccessful at doing that, so, after my futile search, he suggested that I fill the gap myself. I was reluctant because I didn't think I had the gifts or experience to handle such a challenging responsibility. However, due to the rector's persistence, I agreed to take it on in hopes that, with the Lord's help, I could figure it out over time.

Over the next five years, we deployed lots of "tried and true" approaches to introduce people to the Lord—and they all failed miserably. If I had been the rector, I would have fired me. We eventually stopped trying to duplicate the strategies of all the experts and instead started prayerfully listening to the Lord. One step at a time, a process began to fall into place that would go on to help scores of people find fulfillment in their spiritual lives.

The material in this book came to reality in the winter of 2012 in the form of a short follow-up course for interested people who had attended our first January Guest Month at Apostles church. On a humorous note, during that guest month outreach, when we were inviting any and all interested people to attend this introductory course on the Christian faith (at the time called "Christianity Explored," and later changed to "Christianity Examined"), this so-called entry-level course didn't exist!

In the weeks that followed, under the pressure of a weekly deadline, the Lord gave me the concepts, principles, and insights that caused what we needed to take shape. Through that first session, we were literally making it up as we went. Since that time, though the core content of the material has gone through revisions, it has essentially not changed. Sometimes God gives you something to say to help people, and our role is to say it in the best possible way we can and leave the results to Him. The message of this book is not human in origin—whatever quality is in this book belongs to the Lord of the harvest, who is on a rescue mission to heal people from the awful effects of their sinful separation from him.

Since the inception of this course, I have personally witnessed its effects on people in about a hundred teaching sessions. Participants consistently found themselves walking away with a better understanding of the good news that Jesus Christ came to bring. The most common comment usually went like this: "Why haven't I heard it put this way before?" Many realized they were standing at a distance in reaction to a caricature or misconception of the gospel. Once these various misconceptions had given way to clarity of understanding, many were motivated to draw closer to the gospel, and a good number eventually embraced it. For many, "Christianity Examined" became "Christianity Reconsidered." Once they correctly understood it, they had to recalibrate how they had reacted to it, realizing they had previously rejected a false version of it. For many who had a skewed understanding of

Christianity, they gave it a second look—and were glad they did.

So much interest was generated that we eventually developed a series of follow-up courses that now run more than two and a half years to help people grow into a functional understanding of the Christian life as it is taught in the Bible. We call this process "the pipeline." About 90 percent of people who go through the initial Christianity Examined course commit to go through part or all of the optional follow-up courses. Watching people go from little to no prior knowledge of the Bible to a healthy understanding of all that God has for them is the greatest of experiences for a pastor. Those who emerge radically changed for the better are truly my joy and crown. You will read several of their stories in this book.

One of the main things that has been impressed upon us through the years is that the pathway to a healthy faith in the true God has most often started with this Christianity Examined course. Hence, in hopes of making it available to a broader number of people, I have undertaken the challenge of putting it into the book form that you are now holding. In all of our efforts over the last twenty years to create a place for inquiring people to go who are looking for help in how to have a right relationship with God, Christianity Examined has been the centerpiece of it all.

One final important note: in the writing of this book, I wanted a more captivating title for what the gospel is. "Christianity Examined" remains what the course (and book) are about, but I now feel a stronger title is *The Greatest Offer.*

So, with pleasure, I commend to you this book: *The Greatest Offer.*

OPENING REFLECTIONS

My maternal grandfather migrated to America from Sicily in the early 1900s. He came to this country along with millions of other European immigrants. He came over alone on a ship while still in his teens and, due to an oversight, almost did not make it into the country. Here is how it happened.

When he departed from his homeland, he did not understand that he needed a sponsor in America to identify him when he arrived to allow him to pass through customs. After the ship had docked, he was terrified when he realized that he faced a huge, insurmountable obstacle. He did not know anyone in America who could sponsor him and, unless that requirement was met, he would have to stay on the ship and return home. In the providence of God, he had made friends with a fellow traveler on the voyage who had a brother already in America who was going to sponsor him. This man suggested that maybe his brother could also sponsor my grandfather. This was arranged and at least appeared to be a possible solution—but not one without its challenges.

The rule was that the immigrant was put in a line with several other men, and the sponsor had to pick him out of that lineup to confirm that the sponsor had a relationship with the immigrant. This potential sponsor and my grandfather had no prior knowledge of each other, so the chances that the sponsor would make the right selection was a complete roll of the dice. So, when the time came for this to happen, this stranger to my grandfather stood before a long line of immigrants and, after surveying the entire group, randomly walked directly to my grandfather, called him by name, hugged him, and welcomed him to America. The crisis passed, and with this obstacle overcome, my ancestors rooted themselves in American soil over the last century. Talk about hit or miss!

Though it worked out miraculously, this approach is not highly recommended. Sometimes I wonder if this is not the random way many people go through life, including how they adopt their beliefs about God. Often, without carefully thinking things through, people randomly back into a set of beliefs about God. On many occasions, when I ask people how they came up with these beliefs, it's simply hit or miss. However, during my forty-five years as a pastor, I have found through hundreds of spiritual conversations that there is one thing that most everyone agrees on: what a person believes about God is the most life-defining decision they will ever make. In very definitive ways, it affects not only this life but the life to come. Is it wise to approach this hugely impactful issue in a random, whimsical, hit-or-miss way?

The God-question is complex, and given the busyness of life, who has the time and expertise to sort it all out in a reasonable way within a reasonable time frame? Plus, if someone takes this question on, where do they start, and how do they go about it?

The purpose of this book is to assist those with inquiring minds and hearts to examine and perhaps reconsider the

Christian faith in comparison to alternative belief systems and then make an informed choice on what they believe about God and why.

This approach leads to what I think is a very good question: "Why start with Christianity?" Because, according to experts, Christianity, more so than all other faith systems, is a faith that is evidentially verifiable. Unlike others, the central personalities and events that make up Christianity are all a part of a history that stretches over an incredibly long period of time—literally, across millennia. The Bible records that certain people lived in particular places, performed detailed acts, assumed specific roles, and left indelible marks on human history. The Bible is filled with accounts of real people living in real time doing real life in real places which are historically demonstrable.[1]

Once the evidence for Christianity is examined and its historicity established (assuming it is, and will be), it can then be used to measure alternative faith systems against it. So, given its evidential nature, it makes sense that Christianity is a logical starting point and, after all, most people agree that the examination process has to start somewhere.

Lydian stone was a dense type of rock used by the ancient Greeks to test the purity of precious metals like gold and silver. Thus it became a touchstone from which the authenticity of other metals was evaluated. Because of its evidentiary nature, Christianity can be referred to as the Lydian stone, or the touchstone, of faith systems.

A touchstone is a solid black stone with streaks of gold on it to show the purity of the gold. It is a basaltic extrusive rock:

dense, hard, and black. In ancient times, the authenticity and purity of gold was identified by scratching on the touchstone.[2]

Since the starting point will be the Christian faith, how can that faith be best summarized in a simple, understandable way? Here is a good faith effort: Christianity is . . .

"The *greatest* person
with the *greatest* gift
of the *greatest* benefit
to the *greatest* number of people
through the *greatest* offer."

Notice that behind this great offer is a great person. Who is that person? What makes this person stand out above all others and makes him someone who can be trusted? In **chapter one** of this book, this great person will be addressed. In **chapter two**, the question of his trustworthiness will be considered. In the **third chapter**, the magnitude of his great gift will be presented. In the **fourth and final chapter**, the stunning benefit—and its implications—are presented. Finally, in **conclusion**, the great offer to the greatest number of people is explained.

Somewhere along the way, a wise sage noted that "comparison is the mother of all clarity." This proverb has no definitive origin, but it resonates in human experience. While this book will focus on the Christian faith as a starting point, aspects of other religions will be referenced for comparison purposes to show the distinctions that exist among the major faith systems. To be sure, there are similarities, particularly in ethics, in which respect for one's neighbor is emphasized. Religion in general puts forth appeals to a standard of noble, human behavior that cares for others. However, it is equally fair to say that differences do exist and that these often-minimized differences must not be overlooked.

In our culture, it is generally accepted that all religions are essentially the same. Upon close examination, however, it becomes obvious that they had different founders, different assumptions, different teachings, and point to very different destinations. As author and theologian G.K. Chesterton suggested, to reach clarity about what to believe in and why, these comparative distinctions should be brought into the examination process and allowed to stand.

As noted earlier, there is a tendency in today's busy world for people to casually adopt beliefs without fully thinking through their implications. A belief that a certain thing is true implies that its opposite is not true. In philosophical terms, "A" cannot be equal to "anti-A." Perhaps you have heard the term "defeater beliefs." These are beliefs which, if true, overrule or "defeat" contradictory or opposing beliefs. What is not often realized is that to hold to one belief makes contrary beliefs seem implausible. For instance, if you believe that the earth is flat, that rules out any possibility of sailing around the world on a cruise ship. If a person believes that the human body will always heal itself over time, that person will not take medicine and will avoid being admitted to a hospital.

One of the most accepted beliefs today is that all religions are equally valid and basically teach the same thing. This is best captured in the popular "Coexist" symbol.

Stop and think about this for a minute. Islam teaches that there is one God, Allah ("the God"); Hinduism teaches that there are multiple gods (including Shiva, Vishnu, and Brahman); and Buddhism does not affirm the existence of an ultimate God at all. Basic common sense would dictate that these are contradictory teachings and, according to even the most basic rule of logic (the law of non-contradiction), cannot all be true. Essentially, what a person believes implies what they do not believe. So here is a timely warning to our "tolerance culture" that embraces the presupposition that all beliefs are equally true and valid: this is not logically defensible. Therefore, care should be exercised in the embrace of beliefs without fully grasping their full implications.

Embracing a set of beliefs about God, the most important of all subjects, requires careful examination and thoughtful reflection. Therefore, this book will contrast the views and beliefs of various faith systems in the pursuit of clarity that comes from logical consistency.

Reading this book will resemble putting together a jigsaw puzzle. Natalie, my oldest daughter, and I have put together many puzzles during holidays and vacations. Emptying the box of its pieces at the beginning of the process is usually accompanied by an overwhelmed feeling while staring at the mountain of random pieces and trying to figure out where to start. Then, as the end and corner pieces are identified and connected to each other, the framework begins to take shape. Bit by bit, the prominent patterns are discerned and, as they begin to fill out, the finished product can be envisioned. However, along the way, mental walls of frustration and fatigue are encountered such as when a certain piece cannot be found to complete a section, or a certain piece just does not fit where it appears it should be a perfect fit. But by pushing ahead, excitement builds as the picture emerges and momentum surges to finish the project. Loss of sleep is a given at this point. Finally, there is a rare moment of deep satisfaction when the final piece is pressed into place and the deal is done. Strike up the band! Yay, we did it! Glory hallelujah! We relish the joy associated with a huge sense of accomplishment.

The search for God is like putting together a puzzle, overwhelming at points and with moments of exasperation along the way, but well worth the effort once it is all over. Contrary to this exhilaration, there is a low feeling associated with starting but not finishing a puzzle, a feeling of failure about all the time wasted. Perhaps you have heard it said that what you get by achieving your goals is not as important as what you become by achieving your goals. If you are willing to see this search through to its completion, you will be extremely glad you did, and if the message of this book resonates in your heart, you will be shocked at what you will become!

It has been observed, "We live in a package culture that despises content." I think this statement summarizes well the human struggle to burrow past appearance and dig down into substance. A philosopher once said, "The only way to understand anything is by knowing what that thing is."[3]

For those who are serious about coming to an informed conclusion about life's most defining subject, the subject of God, and how to enter into an authentic relationship with him, this book is for you. However, do begin with this encouragement in mind: in order to put the entire puzzle together, you will need to read it all the way to the end.

Next, Session 1: The Greatest Person -- His Uniqueness

ONE

The Greatest Person: His Uniqueness

You are at the beginning of a guided tour of inquiry in which the evidence and rationality of the Christian faith will be examined. As stated in the opening sections, this examination process is greatly enhanced by the fact that Christianity is woven into history, which makes it verifiable. Multiple major events recorded in the Bible are historical in nature. These well-known events—such the parting of the Red Sea, the collapse of the walls of Jericho, the birth of Jesus (celebrated around the world as Christmas), the death of Jesus (known as Good Friday), and the resurrection of Jesus (Easter Sunday)—are all interlaced with history and can be shown as true through the corroboration of a variety of sources.

The initial course that led to this book was titled "Christianity *Examined*." *Examine* is a forensic term frequently used in a legal system context. When used in the legal sense, the term is applied in reference to the investigation of evidence. The examination process includes these steps: first, the collection of relevant data and information; then, the organization of that data into a logical framework; and finally, reaching a conclusion in the form of a verdict. How do judges and juries in the legal system reach conclusions about the cases that come before them daily? They closely examine the evidence.

The aim of this book is to walk readers through an investigative process of Christianity. For clarification purposes, other faith systems will be referenced, and this will frame helpful comparisons and distinctions among the major world religions and their founders. This will indirectly address common questions such as, "Are all faith systems alike?" and "Do all faith systems lead to the same god?"

Perhaps the best vantage point to begin is with a thirty-thousand-foot "panoramic view" from above. A close look at world religions reveals that they cluster in three branches.

First, there are the faith systems that are called *monotheistic* religions. The word monotheism refers to a single god. The monotheistic religions believe that **God is in the foreground.** The monotheistic faiths place the idea of a single god front and center with the challenge that adherents are to center their lives around that single god. The principal monotheistic religions are *Judaism, Christianity*, and *Islam*. In the same way that Christianity stands upon the shoulders of Judaism, Islam stands upon the shoulders of Christianity. So, there is a relationship between these three faiths in that they build upon one another, beginning with the Old Testament writings.

The second group is called *philosophical* religions. These religions place **God in the background**. Though the idea of God is part of their thinking, it is not central to the beliefs nor the behavior of the adherents. Philosophical religions include *Hinduism, Buddhism,* and Eastern philosophies like *Confucianism, Taoism,* and *Shintoism.*

Finally, there is a third branch of faith systems that are called *no-God beliefs.*

This group of religions does not believe in an independent, personal god or a god of any kind. These belief systems teach what I call "God within or not at all." These religions include *new age, agnosticism,* and *atheism.*

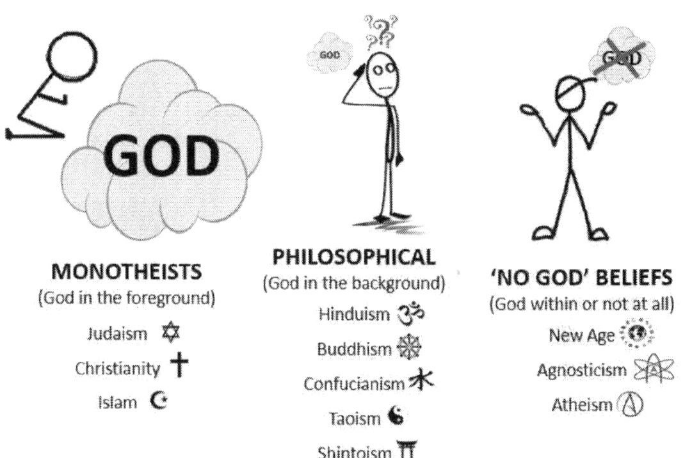

If you prefer a car/truck analogy, monotheist religions allow God to ride in the front seat of the vehicle, philosophical religions put God in the back seat of the car, and "no god" religions don't allow God in their mode of transportation at all.

From this brief summary of major religions, let's move to consideration of their founders as they appeared in history.

The first is Abraham, the founder of Judaism; he was originally called Abram. His name means "father of a multitude." Abraham probably existed in the era around 1700 B.C.

Roughly a millennium later, a cluster of new religions were founded. Among them is Buddhism, which was founded by Buddha, whose name means "enlightened one." There are different branches of Buddhism. Some adherents state that it is incorrect to refer to Buddhism as a religion because they have no defined belief in a god. Confucius (K'ung Fu Tzu), a contemporary of Buddha, founded Confucianism and is often referred to as "the master teacher." Confucius taught filial piety in the surrounding region of China and advocated a type of belief system composed of morals and ethics. Like Buddha, he had no defined belief about God. Lao-tzu, the founder of Taoism (also known as Daoism), was a Chinese contemporary of Confucius. Taoism has many gods, and many of these were borrowed from other cultures. While Confucianism is focused on societal ethics, Taoism is concerned with nature.

A strict chronology now brings us to Christianity, which was founded by the person of Jesus Christ. The name Jesus means "savior," which refers to his identity, and the name Christ means "anointed messiah," which refers to his mission.

Finally, there is one more famous religious founder to be referenced, and that is Mohammad, founder of Islam. This faith system emerged around six centuries after the coming of Christ, and Mohammad viewed himself as the final and ultimate prophet of God.

Zooming in from this panoramic overview, Christianity will be examined along with three pillar beliefs that underpin the entirety of this religion and point to the exceptionality of Jesus. These pillar beliefs are directly linked to the three great Christian feast days celebrated annually. The first is Christmas, followed by Good Friday, and finally Easter. Each of these feast days honors a defining, real-time historical event in the life of Christ, and each is consistent with his life mission and shaped his life message. These events are well known, but what is not known or understood are underlying principles that flow out of them. These three pillar principles define Christianity and explain what it is and how it operates. They also begin to sketch out the uniqueness of Christianity and its founder, Jesus Christ.

PILLARS OF CHRISTIANITY

The first major feast day is Christmas, and this date commemorates the birth of Christ, the beginning event of his earthly life. The season surrounding this special day is called Advent, meaning "arrival." This feast day sets forth the stunning reality that God appeared in human form, and this intervention into our world is called the incarnation.

Many people alive today remember how history was dramatically made on July 20, 1969, when man set foot upon the moon. But how much more dramatic was it when, just more than two thousand years ago, God set foot upon the earth? Down through history, many men have wanted to be god, but only one God has ever wanted to be man. Jesus took the form of a baby,

Down through history, many men have wanted to be god, but only one God has ever wanted to be man.

born of a virgin in fulfillment of a famous Old Testament prophecy: "Behold, a virgin will be with child and bear a son, and she will call his name Immanuel" (Isaiah 7:14, New American Standard Version). The effects of this breathtaking event reverberate not merely in years, but in centuries, with consequences for all mankind. So the first major event is Christmas, celebrating the incarnation, and out of the incarnation flows this key principle that is unique to the person of Jesus, distinctive among all religious founders.

Jesus was the only religious founder who not only pointed to the ideal of spiritual perfection, but claimed that he *himself* was the ideal.

PRINCIPLE NUMBER ONE

Jesus was the only religious founder who not only pointed to the ideal of spiritual perfection but was himself spiritual perfection, the ideal, the only sinless life the world has known.

Many other religious founders had an ideal of a mature spirituality that they conceptualized in a variety of ways. Though they strove—some, very passionately—for their ideal, they never reached that point themselves. In other words, they attempted to lead their followers to an ideal that they themselves never reached. But Jesus, unlike other religious founders, not only pointed to the mountaintop of spiritual perfection, he *was* that mountaintop. He was the perfect embodiment of the spiritual perfection he wanted his followers to attain. It was not an ideal he simply pointed to; he was heavenly, spiritual perfection on full earthly display, and this had its inception at his conception.

The implications of this are staggering. If Jesus was the embodiment of spiritual perfection, what did that look like in human experience? First, Jesus owned his perfection as evidenced in his question to his detractors: "*Which one of you convicts me of sin?*" (John 8:46). Jesus also posed not only as one who was spiritually perfect, but also as one who had a perfect sense of union with the God who sent him to earth. Eastern religions often speak of being one with the gods they recognize and follow, or being one with nature. Jesus represented himself as having a perfect sense of unity with God, his Father. He said, "I and the Father are one" (John 10:30). So Jesus claimed to personify perfection not only in terms of character but also in terms of his relationship with God in Heaven.

Imagine what it would be like to be "up close and personal" with someone who is perfect. What would it have been like to have that perfect person as your oldest brother who always did everything in a way that thrilled your parents? Imagine being around a person who always excelled in whatever they took on? Straight A+ marks throughout school, grades one through twelve? From early in the morning to late in the evening, this person performs everything with the highest level of excellence. In the gospel of Mark, the crowds who followed Jesus were utterly astonished at the way he handled himself, saying, "He does all things well [with excellence]." It would seem impossible not to resent that person even just a little, right? Plus, one would have to deal with the constant exasperation of not measuring up to him no matter how much they tried. A perfect person would expose flaws in others and make everyone around them feel like failures.

Let's consider some other, similar considerations.

- Jesus was spiritually perfect and never had to withdraw or modify any statement he ever made.
- Jesus never once apologized for anything he said . . . because everything he said was always true and rightly stated.
- He never made mistakes and never had to correct himself due to his perfection.
- Jesus never confessed a sin because he never committed any; perfect people do not sin.
- Jesus never attempted to justify his ambiguous behavior, especially to his detractors. He just allowed time, and the plan of God, to unfold, ultimately justifying him and consistently putting him in a good light.
- Jesus never asked anyone to pray *for* him. He encouraged people to pray to him and with him, but not to pray for him.
- Jesus had a perfect balance of personality, with no strong points or weak points, but embodying perfect symmetry.
- Jesus never sought forgiveness, though he often granted it. That all people need forgiveness is implied in the long-held saying, "To err is human, and to forgive is divine." Jesus embodied the only sinless life the world has known. Unlike any other religious founder, he was perfection incarnate.

In his fine book *The Incomparable Christ,* Oswald Sanders relates a fascinating story of a man who was in the Brahmin

Caste of the Hindu religion in India. Christianity began making inroads in his part of the country, which frustrated him greatly, and he became determined to slow down and hopefully stop the conversion rates of Hindus to Christianity. This would be his strategy: the man became a diligent student of the life of Christ as depicted in the Bible. His intent was to find imperfections and flaws in the person of Jesus and then write a pamphlet that would expound why a person would never want to put their faith in someone like Jesus, who had so much failure and weakness in his life.

For the next eleven years, this man studied the New Testament and everything it said about Jesus. In the end, he could not find any flaws or weaknesses in Jesus . . . and came to realize that the person he was trying to find fault in was a person who had no faults. In fact, this skeptical Brahman became convinced that Jesus was who he said he was, the son of God, and became a follower of him.[4]

The second great feast day to be considered in the life of Christ is Good Friday. This feast day commemorates the death of Jesus by crucifixion. As in Christmas, a key principle flows from this feast day. And this principle comes directly from the execution of Jesus.

PRINCIPLE NUMBER TWO

Jesus Christ is the only founder of a religion who posed not only as the model of what he taught, but also as the savior of those he taught.

The principle is in effect an enigma, something which, on the surface, is a confusing statement. Read/consider it again: Jesus was not only the *model* of what he taught, he was the

Jesus was the only religious founder who posed, not only as a model to his followers, but also the savior of his followers.

savior of those he taught. He came to do something that no founder of any other religion ever did. Jesus came to die. He did not just come to teach. He did not just come to heal. The Bible is replete with examples of Jesus healing the sick, giving sight to the blind, restoring lepers to health, and even raising people from the dead. But the central theme of the life of Jesus is not his life, but his *death*. Other religious founders strived to live a noble life, one worth emulating, and certainly Jesus' life was that. But his death is the focal point of his earthly existence.

Note that the deaths of the other religious founders came about as a matter of natural course. Abraham died at the ripe old age of one hundred and seventy-five and was said to be satisfied with life (Genesis 25:7, 8). Confucius also died of old age, disillusioned that so few people were following his teach-

He came to do something that no founder of any other religion ever did. Jesus came to die. He did not just come to teach. He did not just come to heal.

ing. Buddha died peacefully at 80 years of age after having a physical reaction to a bowl of wild, poisonous mushrooms. And Mohammad died a slow death years after being fed a poisoned meal of lamb by a Jewish woman in a city he had conquered. There is no official record available today with any details of the death of Lao-tzu.

These religious founders all died by accident, natural processes, or attempted homicide. In contradistinction to them, however, Jesus died at a young age, laying down his life with full intentionality. Have you ever wondered why a person like Jesus, who went about his everyday life doing so much good for others, would die the most horrific death known to the civilization of that day? How could that happen to a benevolent person of such impeccable moral and spiritual stature?

Well, he not only predicted it, he pointed to it as the overarching goal of his life, and even when his disciples tried to stop him, he rebuked them sternly for getting in the way of God's highest and best design for his life. In spite of their shock, protests, and disbelief, Jesus unapologetically reminded his disciples that the central mission of his life was to die a brutal, inhumane death.

The reason for this mission? To atone for the shortcomings of his followers. Jesus was well aware they would never reach the ideal that he represented, that they would fall painfully short, and he died in their place so they would be spared the consequences of their imperfection! In other words, Jesus laying down his life was an act of sacrificial love. And that is why the day Jesus died is reverently, triumphantly, and celebratedly referred to by his followers as Good Friday. The day that Jesus went through the horror of death by crucifixion brought about enormous good. On that day, the imperfections of sinful humans were covered. To put it another way: throughout his life, Jesus embodied perfection. And through his death he became the savior of those who embodied imperfection. Thus, Jesus posed not only as the model of those he taught, but as the savior of those he taught.

The third and final feast day is Easter Sunday. On that day Christians commemorate the most unique event in all of history: the resurrection of Jesus Christ from the dead. Flowing out of the resurrection is this principle: Jesus Christ is the only religious leader who prescribes salvation, not through self-improvement, but through self-abandonment.

This deeply revolutionary principle and its profound implications are routinely misunderstood by millions of people, even by many among those who embrace the Christian faith. We'll share more about this later.

PRINCIPLE NUMBER THREE

Jesus Christ is the only religious leader who prescribes salvation, not through self-improvement, but through self-abandonment.

Abraham died at a ripe old age, satisfied with life, and was buried alongside his beloved wife Sarah (whose death had preceded his) in a cave, in the ancient area of Hebron, which he had purchased for 400 shekels. Confucius died and was buried. It is theorized by some that Lao-tzu wondered off and died with his water buffalo and was never heard from again. Buddha rotted with food poisoning. Mohammad's body is under the carefully guarded Green Dome in Medina. But Jesus Christ rose from the dead. How stupendous is that? If I stood before you and said, "I'm Superman," you would probably say, "Not sure I believe that." But if I took off and flew across the room and back, I might have your attention. You might just think for a second: *Hmm. There is something different about this guy that he can defy gravity by floating through the air.*

When I was in high school there was a football player who went to the college that I later graduated from, the University of Alabama. He came to be known as "Broadway Joe." His real name was Joe Namath, and, right out of college, he became the starting quarterback for the New York Jets. In January 1969, the Jets were huge underdogs in Super Bowl III, professional football's championship game. One day while talking to sportswriters in the press buildup to the game, Namath did the unthinkable. He not only predicted but actually guaranteed that his outmanned team would win the Super Bowl. To say that the press went completely hysterical over Namath's "guarantee" of a victory would be one of the chief understatements of the twentieth century. There is no way the lowly New York Jets were going to beat the highly talented Baltimore Colts that year. But then, on January 9, 1969, the game was played in Miami, Florida, and lo and behold, the nineteen-and-a-half-point underdog New York Jets remarkably walked off the field as champions of the Super Bowl, victorious over the mighty

Colts, who seemed the much better team. The sports world was completely stunned and, overnight, Joe Namath became a sensation, a sports legend at age 25. Not just because he did the improbable and the unthinkable, but because he did it after predicting it. He truly "shook up the world."

Jesus did something way beyond what Joe Namath did. He rose from the dead after repeatedly predicting he would do so. The Jets winning Super Bowl III back in 1969 was improbable; Jesus rising from the dead was impossible. His resurrection is the clearest proof that Jesus was more than just a person—it was proof that he was God and his resurrection from the dead the indisputably convincing evidence.

Isn't it interesting that we never refer to Jesus as the "late" Jesus? Each year, in the month of November, documentaries usually surface on the death of President John F. Kennedy, who was killed tragically on November 22, 1963. Two other famous men, C.S. Lewis and Aldous Huxley, died on the same day, but the death of Kennedy so overshadowed the deaths of those other famous people that their passing was hardly noticed. It seems as if there is a perpetual fascination with the life and death of the late John F. Kennedy.

A few years ago, while in Dallas, Texas, I went to the Dallas Book Depository, the building from which assassin Lee Harvey Oswald fired the fatal shots that killed the president. I was struck by the long lines of people wrapped around the building waiting to get into the museum even though the event had occurred so many decades ago. We have this intrigue about the "late" John F. Kennedy and the "Camelot" years (as so many called them) that he and his wife Jacqueline were in the White House.

But have you ever noticed that, in reference to Jesus, who died a much more tragic death than Kennedy, we never speak of him as the "late" Jesus? Because he is the resurrected Jesus, people instinctively refer to him as a living person. We do not refer to him in the past tense as we do Kennedy and other deceased people, but in the present tense. Between Good Friday and Easter Sunday, Jesus may actually have been referred to as "the late Jesus" by his devastated followers. But after Easter Sunday, Jesus was from that point forward referred to as the *resurrected Lord Jesus*. His resurrection is the most clear, convincing, and compelling evidence that Jesus was more than just a man. The resurrection, coupled with his prediction of it, is further evidence that he is who he claims to be: not only the son of God, but also God the son.

His resurrection is the most clear, convincing, and compelling evidence that Jesus was more than just a man.

It is profitable to pause here and consider how the events in the final days of Jesus' life form a pattern for how a personal relationship with God works. It is a paradigm of death, burial, and resurrection. If we are going to have a relationship with God, our old self and our efforts to earn the favor of God must die and be buried. In place of that old self, God raises up a resurrected new self. That is what the term "born again" in Scripture implies. When the old man dies, God infuses his life-giving presence into a person so that the fullness of God and the life of God begin to flow in and through that person's life. So, through his death and resurrection, Jesus establishes

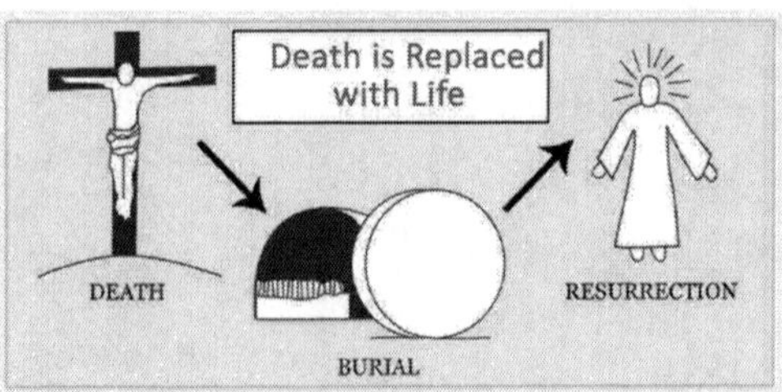

The pattern of death, burial, and resurrection is the pattern for us to follow that leads to salvation.

- **Death** – the old self has to be turned away from
- **Burial** – complete abandonment
- **Resurrection** – Jesus gives new life in place of the old

the pattern in which we lay aside the old man, bury him, and then, in his place, God positions a new, resurrected person. And the Bible says that the Spirit that raised Jesus from the dead is the very same Spirit that raises up a person out of their deadness. We'll share more about this later.

When you compare other religious systems with Christianity, what is the best way to distinguish them? In response to this question, an unknown but wise and insightful person once said: Religion is man's efforts to get to God while Christianity is God's efforts to get to man. That is the fundamental difference.

Finally, is there any place in sacred writings that depicts the relationship of Jesus to other religions? In other words, is there a recorded instance that suggests how the constellation of Christianity and all other faith systems will take shape in the end?

Is there a recorded instance that suggests how the constellation of Christianity and all other faith systems will take shape in the end?

I would suggest that there is one event that occurred soon after the time of Jesus' birth that offers some insight into this question. Early in the account of Matthew's gospel (written account of the life of Jesus), it is reported that a mysterious group of people named *magi* arrived unexpectedly one day in Jerusalem looking for a newborn baby who was reported to be the King of the Jews. Guided by a heavenly star, these men had journeyed from their homeland, in the East, to Jerusalem, the capital city of Israel, in search of this child. When they arrived on the scene, they inquired about where this new king of the Jews could be found. No one in Jerusalem seemed to know! However, the religious leaders were aware of a prophetic Messianic reference in the Old Testament to Bethlehem as the birthplace of this king.

So the local king, Herod, took the magi aside and directed them to this small village south of Jerusalem with these instructions: "Go search for this new king and, once you find him, let me know so I can honor him also." This obscure group of people called the magi, from the East, most likely represented the Eastern religions of that day, which included Hinduism and Buddhism. Off they went to find Jesus, and it is recorded that when they found him, they bowed down and worshipped him. (By the way, sensing Herod's duplicity, they did not report back to him, but steered around Jerusalem when they headed back east for their homes.)

By definition, worship is intended and reserved for God alone. I have been married for more than forty years. I cherish my wife, Cindy, but I do not worship her. I have two daughters, now in their thirties. I am fascinated by them as they are making their way into life and creating their unique impact on the world. I am proud of them and excited for them, but I do not worship them. As these likely representatives of Eastern religions bowed down to worship the baby Jesus, they were in effect confirming, through the supernatural leading of God, the deity of Jesus. And from this incident in the Bible there is a Christmas holiday season greeting that is my favorite of all: "Wise men still seek him."

* * * * *

Small Group Interaction

PERSONAL STORY: VON

I am from the country of Laos, raised in a family of four kids in a religious tradition that did not celebrate Christmas. Christmas to me was someone else's holiday, and I didn't have a clue why they celebrated it.

Therefore, as a family growing up, but now in America, we had nothing to do with Christmas. When my family came to this country, the celebration of Christmas here was new and strange. Our first impression was that Christmas had no spiritual significance but was more of a national holiday like the

Fourth of July—more of a commercially driven Christmas but not in any way a Christ-centered celebration. We did not connect Christ to the Christmas season at all. Eventually, we got caught up in the cultural expression of Christmas but had no connection to its spiritual meaning.

Later, in adulthood, I developed a desire to go to church but didn't know why. At first I was discouraged by those around me from going, so I did not act upon that desire until I met Rob, my husband. He invited me to attend church. My initial response was one of indifference. I just wasn't sure what to make of it, but gradually church came to feel like home. Though I eventually became comfortable in church, I still did not feel fully comfortable in my relationship with God. This distant feeling continued until I attended a short course on what it means to have a personal relationship with him. The course was called Christianity Examined. It was there that I realized God wanted a relationship with me, and that he had given his Son to bridge us together by his death on the cross. I became a Christian. Like the magi, I became a worshiper of Jesus.

Once I had connected all the dots, in time Christmas took on a whole new meaning, especially when I saw Christmas through the eyes of a mother. Knowing how much Kinsie, my daughter, meant to me and how fiercely protective I am of her, I realized the magnitude of God's love expressed toward us by giving his only child to die for us.

I also realized that by receiving the gift of Jesus, I had received the gift that keeps on giving so many other valuable things: joy and peace in my relationship with God, love for others, and hope for my future in eternity.

So, comparing the emptiness and hollowness of my childhood view of Christmas to the fullness and richness of my experience of Christmas now is like going from nothing to everything. And now that Kinsie has Jesus in her heart, Christmas has also become so much more meaningful for us as a family since we experience it together with genuine intentionality. The experience of God's love together as a family only serves to multiply the joy, peace, and hope that Jesus came to give every human heart.

REFLECTION QUESTIONS

- What part of the presentation on Jesus' uniqueness most caught your attention (made the deepest impression, struck you the most, or created the most tension within you)?
- What observations, thoughts, or questions might you have about the uniqueness of Jesus?
- What impact would you say the uniqueness of Jesus might have on your spiritual journey?
- What aspect of Von's story was most meaningful to you?
- Invite the group to explain the difference between religion and Christianity.

Group Interactions with the Three Core Principles of Jesus' Uniqueness

- "Jesus was the only religious founder who not only pointed to an ideal; he was the ideal." ***What is so risky about setting oneself up as an ideal for others to follow?***
- "Jesus was the only religious founder who posed, not only as a model to his followers, but also as the savior of his followers." ***What is so intriguing about Jesus serving in the dual role of model and savior?***
- "Jesus was the only religious founder who prescribed salvation, not through self-improvement, but through self-abandonment." ***If you wanted to explain this concept to your best friend, how would you translate it into your own words?***

Next, Session 2: The Greatest Person -- The Reliability of His Word

TWO

The Greatest Person: The Reliability of His Word

Can I ask you to ponder this question: *Who is the greatest person you have known?* Please answer, at least in your own mind, before continuing to read.

Our examination of Christianity began by looking at the uniqueness of Jesus. Noted were three insights that correspond to the three great Christian feast days that distinguish Jesus from all other religious founders. The first feast day is Christmas, which commemorates the incarnation of Jesus, and the principle drawn from Jesus' incarnation is that he is the only religious founder who pointed not only to an ideal of spiritual perfection but *was* the ideal. He was God. The second feast day is Good Friday, which points to the crucifixion, and from the crucifixion a second principle emerges: that Jesus is the only founder of a religion who posed not only as a *model* of what he taught, but as the *savior* of those he taught. The third feast day is Easter Sunday, which commemorates the resurrection of Jesus, and from that event issues a final principle that

Jesus is the only religious founder who prescribed salvation, not through self-enhancement or through self-improvement, but through self-abandonment.

These three pillar insights are interwoven throughout the Christian faith, and together they form a foundation upon which one can build a case for the uniqueness of Jesus and Christianity.

Referring back now to the opening question of this chapter, answer this query: *What is unique about whoever came to mind as the greatest person you have known?* I am sure that person was very distinct, but in what sense were they unique? What makes people great is that they have traits that are common to others but in *greater degrees* than others (intelligence, looks, strength, athleticism). On the other hand, Jesus was unique in the sense that he possessed traits no other person had. He was unlike any other person, and no other person was ever like him.

By way of summary, then, stated simply, Christianity is . . .

"The *greatest PERSON*
with the *greatest gift*
of the *greatest benefit*
to the *greatest number* of people
through the *greatest offer.*"

In chapter one, the uniqueness of this person behind the offer of this great gift was considered in detail. Moving beyond the uniqueness of Jesus, a related question arises: "How does a person begin to relate to this remarkably intriguing person named Jesus, and how can one be sure that he is trustworthy?"

First, it helps to broaden the question and ask: "How does a relationship between any two people begin?"

This is a fascinating question that deserves a meaningful answer. First, it helps to broaden the question and ask: "How does a relationship between any two people begin?" Relationships begin and develop when the parties involved commit to the process of self-revelation. Self-revelation, or self-disclosure, is the act of revealing one's inner personal world to another. It is essential to all relational health and development. In other words, a person must be willing to be known by others to experience connection with others. Opening oneself up to another is the raw material from which connection is built. Therefore, a person must make the investment of self-revelation for a relationship to be conceived and to gestate.

Let me illustrate the point. When I teach this concept in a live setting, I usually ask a person in the audience whom I have never met to come forward and participate in an exercise. I set up two chairs at the front of the room and ask the volunteer to sit next to me in one of the chairs. The first thing I ask the volunteer to clarify is that we have never met, and that a relationship prior to this moment does not exist.

The conversation usually goes something like this:

JAMES: Thank you for serving as our volunteer tonight. Let me begin by asking you to clarify that we have never met before, and that we have never had any kind of relationship prior to this moment, right?

VOLUNTEER: No, we have not.

JAMES: My intent is to initiate a relationship with you, and to do that I am going to ask you some general personal questions. Do I have your permission to do that?

VOLUNTEER: Yes, I am open to doing that.

JAMES: Very good. So, here is our M-O—mode of operation—going forward. I am going to ask you a set of ten questions, and on the first time through these questions, you're not allowed to say anything. In other words, I need you to just sit silently as I pose these questions to you, okay?

VOLUNTEER: Sure, if that is what you want me to do.

JAMES: Okay, here we go!

- What is your middle name? (silence, as expected, follows.)
- Where do you live? (Silence. The audience might begin to chuckle a bit.)
- What is your favorite meal of the day? (silence)
- What's your favorite color? (silence)
- What's your favorite restaurant? (silence)
- Who is your best friend? (silence . . . the volunteer may begin to squirm a bit here, as the exchange is fairly awkward.)
- Have you ever had a life-threatening illness? (silence)
- What's your favorite pastime? (silence)

- What's on your bucket list? (silence)
- Do you believe in God? (silence)

Now, turning to the audience, I usually say, "Wouldn't you agree that I asked some interesting questions? But there was no reply, so here is the awkward result. Since the volunteer chose not to reveal anything about themselves by not answering the questions, I do not know any more about this person than when I started, do I? In spite of my very fine questions, still no relationship, right? The reason I don't know any more about this person is because he/she is not practicing self-disclosure."

I turn back to the volunteer and make a second attempt at initiating a relationship.

JAMES: With your permission, I am going to ask you the same questions again, and this time, instead of you answering them, I am going to answer them for you while you again remain silent. I am going to speculate. As I pose the questions to you again, please remain silent. Okay?

VOLUNTEER: Okay.

- What is your middle name? (I wait just a second, then give an "answer.") I will bet it is Lucy.
- Where do you live? . . . I am going to say, Dunwoody.
- What is your favorite meal of the day? . . . I bet it's breakfast.
- What is your favorite color? . . . I think it is brown.

- What is your favorite restaurant here in Atlanta? . . . I'll say Willy's Mexican Grill.
- Who is your best friend? . . . Probably your next-door neighbor.
- Have you ever had a life-threatening illness? . . . From your healthy appearance, I am going to say no.
- What is your favorite pastime? . . . I bet it's bicycle riding on the Silver Comet Trail!
- What is on your bucket list? . . . I think you aspire to do a double back somersault off of Mount Rushmore.
- Do you believe in God? . . . You are not sure, which makes you agnostic.

I turn back to the audience. "Okay, now that I have asked the questions again, but answered them in a speculative way, do I know any more about this person than I did a few minutes ago? She was not given an opportunity to engage in any self-disclosure, and my speculation is a poor substitute for her self-expression. I did succeed in creating an imaginary person, one who exists only in my mind, but this turned out to be just another failed attempt to begin a relationship.

"So, let's do this right this time by asking the questions again, and I'll give our volunteer a chance to respond." I turn back to the on-stage volunteer.

JAMES: I am going to ask you the same questions a third time, and after each question, feel free to answer, okay? (Volunteer nods.)

Tell us, what is your middle name?

VOLUNTEER: Claire.

JAMES: Not Lucy, huh? And, uh, where do you live?

VOLUNTEER: Dunwoody. (The audience might laugh and even clap a bit.)

JAMES: You're kidding. I'm one for two so far. Yay! So, what is your favorite meal of the day?

VOLUNTEER: Brunch.

JAMES: I was close, but close only counts in horseshoes. Okay, what is your favorite color?

VOLUNTEER: Green.

JAMES: Green. Not brown, huh? And your favorite restaurant?

VOLUNTEER: Chick-fil-A.

JAMES: And your best friend?

VOLUNTEER: Victoria.

JAMES: Who is Victoria?

VOLUNTEER: Um, I work with her.

JAMES: Okay, not your next-door neighbor, huh?

VOLUNTEER: No. Sorry.

JAMES: Missed that one too. Have you ever had a life-threatening illness?

VOLUNTEER: No.

JAMES: No, you look very healthy. What is your favorite pastime?

VOLUNTEER: Um . . . reading!

JAMES: Reading. What kind of books do you like to read?

VOLUNTEER: Just like different ones.

JAMES: Mm-kay. And what is on your bucket list? What do you want to do before your life comes to an end?

VOLUNTEER: I really wanna, like, swim with sharks.

JAMES: Excuse me? Please say that again. (Audience typically laughs.)

VOLUNTEER: I wanna swim with sharks.

JAMES: Hello. You want to swim with sharks?

VOLUNTEER: Yeah. I just think they are really cool.

JAMES: Wow! Do your parents know about this? (Again, laughter.)

Last question: do you believe in God?

VOLUNTEER: Yes.

JAMES: Great. How long have you believed in God?

VOLUNTEER: Ever since I was five.

JAMES: How did you first hear about God?

VOLUNTEER: From my family. I mean, I was raised in the church, so . . .

JAMES: Did you find it hard to believe in God as a young person?

VOLUNTEER: Not really, 'cause, um, when I was small, I actually like had this vision of Jesus being in my room.

And he was like, um, "I want you to dedicate your life to me," and to, um, "share my work with others." So from then on, I was like: "Okay, cool."

JAMES: Wow! So how old were you when you had that experience?

VOLUNTEER: I was five.

JAMES: Five years old?

VOLUNTEER: Mm-hmm.

JAMES: Wow. That's pretty exciting. So, tell us your first name.

EMMA: Emma.

JAMES: Emma. All right, so now we all know some interesting things about our new friend Emma. Certainly, more than when we started. She's kind of an intriguing person, wouldn't you say? And, based upon what you have heard, wouldn't you also like to get to know her a little better? So yeah, Emma, by giving us a certain amount of information about yourself, by being open to reveal yourself to us, we now know more about you, and maybe at some point, you'll have the opportunity to talk further with some other people in the room.

All right, great, let's give Emma a nice round of applause. Thank you, Emma. You did a great job.

Based upon that exchange between Emma and I, consider these three scenarios:

Scenario #1: I attempted to get to know Emma. And since she did not respond to any of my get-acquainted questions, her instructions to not disclose anything about herself precluded the development of a relationship. Keep in mind that this is how it would be with God if he chose to communicate nothing about himself to us and left us completely in the dark about who he is, also precluding the possibility of any relationship with him. This scenario leaves us with a distant, futile, and empty feeling inside about the God-question.

Scenario #2: I attempted to create a relationship with Emma by asking her questions and answering them myself. I filled in the answers for her. Though I did succeed in creating a personal profile of her, it was purely imaginary and speculative, and this excluded the possibility of a genuine and authentic connection with the real Emma. Many people commit this same mistake when it comes to God. By not letting the Lord speak for himself, people create an imaginary concept of God, and they cut themselves off completely from any chance of an authentic, personal association with the real and true God.

Scenario #3: In the third and final attempt to initiate a relationship with Emma, she was given the opportunity to respond. She was freed up to exercise honest self-disclosure and reveal things about herself that created a framework to begin a genuine connection with the real Emma. And so it is in our relationship with God. If we refuse to believe he is there and make no effort to listen to him, or if we speculate about who he is and cut him off from his own reality, that precludes a relationship.

Many people create an image of God in their own minds and worship a god of their own imagination, burying the reality of God underneath their personal speculations.

Why not just let God speak for himself since he has revealed himself to us in a variety of ways, including through a written record called the Bible? For any relationship to materialize, one person must initiate or take the first step in hopes that the second party will respond. That is what Jesus did when he came to earth. The astounding fact is that he initiated a relationship with us by revealing both his desire for and the terms of such a relationship. This relational invitation and framework are captured and preserved in a book called the Bible. Now, on face value, this looks very promising: Jesus has stepped forward and done his part by vulnerably opening himself up to us. However, the people whom Jesus is trying to reveal himself to have not all been completely receptive. Instead of giving Jesus a fair chance to express an interest in relating himself to us, so many have given Jesus the cold shoulder. In fact, there is a prevailing and overriding skepticism toward the Bible today that effectively mutes the voice of Jesus and completely shuts down any possibility of a relationship with him. For someone to take the words of another person seriously, we have to trust that the message the other person is trying to get across to us is sincere and real.

Here is where the breakdown lies between Heaven and earth: the Bible is predominantly viewed in Western culture as an untrustworthy book that is not to be taken with any seriousness. Even though the Bible claims to be the Word of God, questions arise as to whether it is an authentic expression of what he is really trying to say to us. This deeply rooted skepticism usually revolves around these two concerns:

- "Is it true that what Jesus said is in the Bible?"
- "And if so, is what Jesus said in the Bible true?"

In other words, does the Bible truly reflect the words Jesus spoke while here on earth? And if that is so, do these recorded words of Jesus accurately reflect the truth? Both are great and relevant questions, and honest seekers of the truth need to decide whether they can be satisfactorily answered. As it stands now, the Bible is the most criticized and least understood book in the world. This prevailing skepticism is often tied to a superficial rather than an evidenced-based determination. Are you in this category, a skeptic? Are you willing to give things a second look? As a former skeptic, may I appeal to you in the strongest ways to re-evaluate your deep questioning in light of the most current evidence available today?

To address this "relationship-precluding" barrier of skepticism, consideration from an evidential standpoint will now be given to the reliability, authenticity, and trustworthiness of the Bible.

If God desires a relationship with us, how could he most effectively communicate his intentions to us? There is an old saying that goes like this: "The weakest of ink is better than the strongest of memory." To preserve the accuracy of ideas in ancient times generationally, the best medium to do that was the written word. Oral tradition was also used in those days, but with less accuracy than the written medium. So it appears that the Lord chose the most accurate option of that day, and men moved by the hand of God transcribed the inspired thoughts of God into the inspired written Word of God. So the Bible makes the claim that it is the primary instrument through which God communicates his heart desire and the terms for a meaningful relationship with him. This astounding claim amounts to the Bible being God's written composition of a love story between himself and the world he has created.

This astounding claim amounts to the Bible being God's written composition of a love story between himself and the world he has created.

But can that claim be substantiated through evidence?

God has revealed himself to us in two primary ways. First, through Jesus, who is the living word; and second, through the Bible, which is the written Word. These are two inseparable realities. It is like trying to remove stain from wood once it has been applied. Trying to separate the two is not possible without damaging the integrity of both.

Why is this true? In the body of instruction Jesus handed down to us, he quoted from twenty-four (roughly two-thirds) of the thirty-nine Old Testament books. The writings of the other nine New Testament authors included quotes from thirty-four Old Testament books. So the Old Testament was Jesus' and the apostolic writers' Bible, and it was thus woven into Jesus' teaching. Like a double-knit fabric with the interlocked knitting of two threads, the two testaments are carefully woven together. So embracing the New Testament means that the Old Testament comes with it, and vice versa.

I once heard a relative say that he believed in the words of Jesus as the authoritative Word of God, but that the rest of the Bible did not fit in that category. Based upon what has just been said about the unity of the Bible with the words of Jesus, his position was untenable.

So, God reveals himself through the living word and the written Word. Why should we equate the Bible with the Word of God? Well, astoundingly, the Bible claims—approximately 2,700 times—to be the Word of God. Is this just fanciful thinking, or can that claim be verified? Many believe that it can, but nonetheless, each individual needs to be convinced by objective evidence, which will now be presented.

CAN WE VERIFY THE BIBLE AS TRUTH?

There are two different approaches one can choose from. The first is the "inside-out approach." It is dependent on what the Bible says about itself. In other words, the Bible claims to be the inspired Word of God, but does that claim alone establish it as true? It has been fairly countered that this self-attesting claim is nothing more than circular reasoning and is not, by itself, a fully convincing argument. For instance, my self-claim to be President of the United States is not enough for me to demand a key to the Oval Office.

The second approach is the "outside-in approach." In other words, what evidence is there outside the Bible that confirms the self-attesting claims of its divine origin? This approach eliminates over-dependence on the self-attesting claim of the

Bible to establish its veracity, and it is this approach that best serves the purpose of this book.

NATURAL EVIDENCE

Consideration will be given to the evidence that exists in the natural realm. One of the most common objections leveled against the Bible goes like this: given the number of times the Bible has been copied over the centuries, surely much of its original content has been lost in the shuffle of the transcription process. Honest scholarship requires that advocates of the Bible admit that its original manuscripts are decomposed, and there is no longer access to them. This means that only copies of the original writings are accessible, but not originals. How big of a problem does this pose? Honest scholarship also requires that it be recognized that the dearth of original manuscripts is not only a challenge to the trustworthiness of the Bible but is a challenge to the trustworthiness of all ancient literature. If the Bible is to be viewed skeptically because of its lack of original manuscripts, then all ancient literature should be viewed with similar skepticism because of its lack of original manuscripts. Fairness requires consistency of concern for not only the Bible but for all writings of antiquity.

To address this challenge, the literary world has established simple but effective criteria to determine the accuracy of ancient literature copies, and there are two guidelines. The first is called *quantity* and the second is called *proximity*. To determine the accuracy of the copies of ancient literature, scholars first determine the quantity of available copies. Then scholars determine how close the copies are to the original manuscripts, which is called proximity.

> Here is a sampling of ancient writings from around the time of Jesus:
>
> Tacitus: This Roman historian wrote *Annals of Imperial Rome* in AD 116. There is *one* existing manuscript, copied about AD 850.
>
> Josephus: The famous Jewish historian wrote *The Jewish War* in the mid-first century, and there are nine copies composed from the ninth, eleventh, and twelfth centuries AD.
>
> Homer's *Illiad*: The original manuscript is dated 800 BC, and there are 650 copies composed a millennium after the original.

With this information in mind, how does the Bible fare when viewed through the categories of *quantity* and *proximity*? Beginning with the New Testament, there is access to more than 5,000 copies, *and the first complete manuscript copies are all within three hundred years of the life of Jesus.* Given this mountainous volume of copies and their close proximity to the New Testament originals, when compared to the minuscule number of copies and the centuries of time lapse between copies of other ancient literature and their originals, the New Testament towers above ancient literature in terms of its accuracy of transcription.

Bruce Metzger, an American biblical scholar of both Greek and New Testament criticism, translator, and longtime professor at Princeton Seminary, and one of the most influential New Testament scholars of the twentieth century, said this in his book *The Text of the New Testament: Its*

Transmission, Corruption, and Restoration about the quantity of New Testament manuscripts: "The quantity of NT [New Testament] material is almost embarrassing in comparison with other works of antiquity."

QUANTITY OF COPIES ISSUE

- Greek manuscripts: 5,664 catalogued copies
- Latin Vulgate manuscripts: there are 8,000 to 10,000
- There are a total of 8,000 in Ethiopic, Slavic, and Armenian
- In all, there are about 24,000 New Testament manuscripts in existence.

The Bible stacks up against other well-known works of antiquity very favorably. There is sound reason to have great confidence in the fidelity with which this material has come down to the current generation, especially when compared with any other ancient literary work. That confidence is shared by distinguished scholars throughout the world. In his book *The New Testament Documents: Are They Reliable?,* the late F.F. Bruce, eminent professor at the University of Manchester, England said, "There is no body of ancient literature in the world which enjoys such a wealth of good textual attestation as the New Testament."[5]

Sir Frederick Kenyon, the former director of the British Museum, has said, "In no other case is the interval of time between the composition of the book and the earliest manuscripts so short as in that of the New Testament." He went on to say, "The foundation for any doubt that the Scriptures have come down to us substantially as they were written has been removed."

Further, there is one other fascinating piece of corollary evidence that strengthens the case for the Bible. It is worth noting that virtually the entire New Testament can be reconstructed from the writings of early church fathers, all who lived within three hundred years of the life of Christ. Amazingly, this enables scholars to do comparative studies between the New Testament copies and the scriptural quotations in the writings of the early church fathers in a check-and-balance process to further validate the accuracy of the New Testament copies. Though variances between the manuscripts exist, none casts any doubt about any fundamental teaching of the Christian faith.

Moving now to the Old Testament, what about the accuracy of the copies of the older portion of the Bible? Well, of course the original manuscripts of the Old Testament have decomposed. They have been long gone, for millennia, and during the era in which the decomposition occurred, there were not sophisticated methods of copying manuscripts. Modern machines, such as copiers, were inconceivable to the people of that day. Given that reality, what assurance is there that the current copies of the Old Testament documents are accurate?

One of the most amazing occurrences in the minds of many modern-day archeologists was the 1947 discovery of the Dead Sea Scrolls. The following is an account of how the discovery unfolded. On an ordinary day, a Bedouin shepherd boy was with his flock close to the city of Qumran right next to the Dead Sea. It happened randomly that, bored while shepherding his flock, the boy picked up a rock and tossed it into one of multiple cave openings on the side of the mountain. When the rock landed inside the cave, it made an unexpected shattering sound, and this, naturally, caught his attention.

So he threw a second rock into the same cave, and it caused the same mysterious breaking sound. This prompted the boy and his companions to scale the side of the mountain and look inside the cave to see what was causing the breaking sound. While doing so, they happened upon a huge quantity of sealed pottery jars. The jars themselves looked very ancient, and yet at the same time ordinary.

Once they were opened, though, what was discovered inside was anything but ordinary. In fact, it was extraordinary. Discovered inside the jars were 972 manuscripts that, theoretically, had been hidden away to protect them from their ancient Roman adversaries. Included in this trove of documents was found *every book in the Old Testament except for the book of Esther.* Incredibly, upon initial discovery, these documents were not recognized as having any value and were almost incinerated. After being taken to a monastery in nearby Jerusalem, however, a knowledgeable person realized that these documents had earmarks of sacred writings and called in linguistic experts. Eventually, they came to the realization that this was an archeological discovery which would shake the world of biblical scholarship.

Included in the Dead Sea Scrolls was an entire reading of the book of Isaiah, the longest Old Testament prophetic book. The oldest copy of the book of Isaiah to that time, called the Masoretic Text, dated about 900 AD! It was then compared to the Isaiah scroll from the Dead Sea discovery, manuscripts dated about 125 BC. Though these two documents had *one thousand years* between them, remarkable similarity was discovered. The two documents looked virtually the same, with only a few minor variations. So now, documentable evidence had been discovered that the Old Testament manuscripts were accurately transcribed through the centuries. This conclusion was not just speculation, but for all eyes to see was hard evidence in the form of the Dead Sea Scrolls. Skeptics and critics who had scorned the accuracy of the copies of Old Testament manuscripts now had to go sit in the corner and be quiet.

And so, after assembling and organizing relevant evidence into a logical framework, the verdict in the case for the trustworthiness of the copies of both the Old and New Testaments is in: according to the experts, the documentable evidence for the historical accuracy of the Bible is vastly superior to all other ancient literature.

SCIENCE

Leaving the world of literary science behind, attention will now be focused on modern science. What evidence can be found in the world of modern science today that would confirm the veracity or truthfulness of the Bible? In recent centuries, the worlds of faith and science have become polarized by the fierce debate between creation and evolution. Originally, the development of the field of modern science was driven by the assumption that life operates in an orderly universe created by a God of order and design. This is called the teleological argument, and it is one of the classic theistic proofs that supports belief in God based upon the design of the universe.

At the time of the origin of modern science in the sixteenth and seventeenth centuries, faith and science were seen as compatible, not adversarial, fields. The founders of modern science were people of faith; these were men like Isaac Newton. But the advent of the widespread belief in evolution in the 1800s spawned a great divorce between the idea of God and the material universe, and the intense debate over evolution versus creationism continues unabated to this day.

Here is a sample of the different, opposing viewpoints among scientists.

A leading atheist today named Richard Dawkins, an evolutionary biologist, claims in his book *The God Delusion*, that a person cannot be an intelligent, scientific thinker and hold any religious belief.[6] However, there are many people in the world of science who would dispute Dawkins's audacious claim.

In fact, in the same year that Dawkins's book was published, a book called *Language of God,* authored by eminent scientist Francis Collins, also was published. In his book Collins writes that he believes the finely tuned beauty and order of nature point to a divine creator. He then goes on to describe his conversion from atheism to Christianity, explaining that his journey from skepticism to belief was driven by scientific evidence.[7]

Nevertheless, this supposedly irreconcilable polarization between faith and science is consistently implied in the secular media today. This media bias is almost always tilted toward the skeptical assumption that the Bible and creationism are outdated, ancient history that are hopelessly out of touch with sophisticated modern-day science. The implication is that no intelligent person would be so foolish as to embrace such fanciful ideas. But previous and current surveys of the beliefs of scientific-minded people suggest otherwise. Two famous studies, done at the beginning and end of the twentieth century, revealed that 40 percent of scientists are skeptics but that there is also an equivalent 40 percent who are people of faith with a strong belief in God. Note the consistency between the two survey results done almost a century apart. This powerfully implies that skepticism did not increase during the 1900s.[8] The cultural elites who want us to think intelligent people can no longer embrace the Bible and Christianity are ignoring the truth that faith and science are not polar opposites but complementary realities.

The scientific realm is inherently technical—to such an extent that it's easy to get lost in the weeds of technicality. So perhaps it is best to keep things simple. In the 1700s, William Paley made this commonsense argument for intelligent design: "Every watch has a watchmaker."

In the same way, the saying goes, "Every portrait has an artist." Therefore, every design has a designer and, by implication, Paley is saying that the best evidence for a creator is the creation itself. Consider the following scenarios from a simple, commonsense perspective.

SCENARIO #1

Sixteen-year-old Johnny comes downstairs from his bedroom on his way to school one morning, and he finds his favorite alphabet cereal box spilled all over the kitchen table. Curiously, the letters form this message: *Don't forget your science project on your way to school this morning.* How did the message get there? Random chance? Or did an intelligent being like his mother put it there? What does your common sense tell you?

SCENARIO #2

Imagine that while you are walking along the beach one day, you spot a diamond-studded Rolex watch on the white sand. What does common sense tell you about how the watch came into existence and about how it ended up on the sandy beach? Is this a product of wind and rain and erosion coming together to suddenly cause this watch to appear out of nowhere? Instead, what common sense tells you is that some really smart person made that watch, and some really careless person dropped it (and is probably out there looking for it).

SCENARIO #3

You are talking with a friend in a coffee shop and they say to you, “Hey, listen up, I have a new theory about how modern-day airplanes came into existence. I’ve concluded that an F5 tornado blew through a junkyard, and out came this brand new, shiny 747 airplane!” You would be a little bit skeptical about this new theory, wouldn’t you? Of course you would.

All of this begs common sense. But evolution advocates urge us to believe that we came into existence in a similar, random way. And yet there are multiple quotes of educated, reasonable, intelligent people who have immersed their lives in the field of science and are of the professional opinion that scientific evidence points back to theism, not atheism.

Here is one example from the field of astronomy. In his book *God and the Astronomers,* Robert Jastrow concludes this about the origin of the universe.

> Science has proven that the universe has exploded into being at a certain moment. It asks, “What cause produced this effect? Who or what put matter into the universe?” Science cannot answer these questions because, according to astronomers, in the first moments of its existence, the universe was compressed to an extraordinary degree and consumed by the heat of a fire beyond imagination. The shock of that instant must have destroyed every particle of evidence that could have yielded a clue to the cause of the great explosion. A sound explanation

> may exist for the explosive birth of our Universe, but if it does, science cannot find out what the explanation is. The scientist's pursuit of the past ends at the moment of creation. This is an exceedingly strange development, unexpected by all but the theologians. They have always accepted the word of the Bible: "In the beginning, God created the heavens and the earth" (Genesis 1:1). So then, it is not a matter of another year, another decade of work, another measurement, or another theory; at this moment it seems as though science will never be able to raise the curtain on the mystery of creation. For the scientist who lived by his faith in the power of reason, the story ends like a bad dream. He has scaled the mountains of ignorance, he is about to conquer the highest peak, [and] as he pulls himself over the final rock, he is greeted by a band of theologians who have been sitting there for centuries."[9]

The *anthropic principle* is a fancy term for the mounting evidence that has many scientists today believing that the universe is a finely tuned reality that is the result of intentional design specifically set up to support human life on planet Earth. There are more than one hundred factors—including the speed of the earth's rotation, the thickness of the earth's crust, water vapor levels in the atmosphere, the speed of light, and the actual tilt of the earth—that must be tuned to very strict levels for human life to be sustained. If you want to read more about this, you can find it in detail in a book called *I Don't Have Enough Faith to Be an Atheist.* So the commonsense argument goes like this: *every design has a designer; the universe has a highly complex design; therefore, the universe has a designer.*

The Bible puts it this way, in Psalm 19:1 of the Old Testament, "The heavens declare the glory of God." Romans 1:20 (New Testament) says, "Since the creation of the world, his invisible attributes and divine nature have been clearly seen through what has been made, so that everyone is without excuse." The Bible makes it plain that, from the beginning, God's invisible attributes and divine nature have been so clearly manifested that skeptics are without a defense for their unbelief.

Let me conclude this section with this statement: the greatest evidence for a creator is the creation itself.

CONCLUSION

After assembling and organizing relevant evidence into a logical framework, the verdict in the field of science for the case of the trustworthiness of the Bible is in: the common-sense reasoning based upon the scientific data for the historical accuracy of the Bible is convincing.

ARCHAEOLOGY

The word *archeology* means the "study of ancient history." It is defined as the study of the human past through the use of material remains. What evidence for the truthfulness of the Bible is "found in the ground"? Here are a few notable examples.

Sir William Ramsey lived from 1851-1939 and is generally accepted as one of the greatest archeologists ever. He was educated in the German liberal schools, which were extremely skeptical about the trustworthiness of the Bible.

He was initially a skeptic of the New Testament book of Acts and eventually decided to go to Asia Minor in hopes of discovering archaeological findings that would undermine the historic accuracy of this prominent biblical book. After thirty long years of archeological spade work, Ramsey, the skeptic, came to this conclusion: "Luke, the author of the book of Acts, was a historian of first rank. Not only are his statements of fact trustworthy, but his authorship should be placed along with the greatest of historians of all time." He also wrote that Luke's history in the book of Acts is unsurpassed in respect to its trustworthiness.[10] Note, especially, that this opinion was expressed by a man who spent three decades trying to discredit a single New Testament book! Instead of deconstructing this book, Ramsey deconstructed his own skepticism and concluded that the book of Acts was true and second to none in terms of accurate biblical history.

A man by the name of Nelson Glueck was an American rabbi. Before his death in 1971, his picture appeared on the cover of *Time* magazine in the December 13, 1963 issue, where he was cited for his significant archaeological discoveries in Israel.

Glueck was an academic, archeologist, and pioneer in the field of biblical archeology. His archeological efforts resulted in the discovery of 1,500 different ancient sites that are mentioned in history and in the Bible. He came to this conclusion: "Not even one archeological discovery has ever countermanded anything in the Bible."[11]

Scores of archeological findings have been made which confirm, in exact detail, historical statements that are found in the Bible. Glueck devoted his professional life to archeological study, and he stated that there has never been a single discovery from archeology that has contradicted the Bible. His conclusion was that an abundance of evidence supporting the Bible's trustworthiness has been "found in the ground."

CONCLUSION

And so, after assembling and organizing relevant evidence into a logical framework, the verdict in the field of archaeology in the case of trustworthiness of the Bible is in: the documentable evidence in this field for the historical accuracy of the Bible is 100 percent validating. This is why archaeology is sometimes referred to as "the Bible's best friend."

SUPERNATURAL EVIDENCE

Leaving natural evidence behind, consideration will now be given to supernatural evidence that supports the truthfulness of the Bible. Let's start with this: how good are you at predicting the future? Have you ever filled out an NCAA March Madness basketball tournament bracket? If you have, the very thought of it brings a smile to your face because you know through experience what an exercise in futility it can be. What are the odds you are going to win if you enter the ESPN NCAA March Madness contest? The odds that you will get the tournament bracket 100 percent correct are 1 in 9.2 quintillion! That is partly why the NCAA tournament is called March Madness: it is madness to try and predict what's going to happen. (It is intriguing that Warren Buffet offers his employees at Berkshire Hathaway a tidy sum of 1 billion dollars to anyone who can come up with the perfect bracket.) However, don't get your hopes up! According to the NCAA, there has never been a verified perfect bracket. Human nature is equipped through memory to reflect on the past, but predicting the future accurately is not within human capability.

Now, what does this have to do with the trustworthiness of the Bible? Here is the connection. Have you heard the term "predictive prophecy"? The term refers to those parts of the Bible that provide clear, specific, and verifiable predictions of future events hundreds of years before they come to pass. The Bible is filled with statements that specify exactly what will happen in the future.

Just how extensive is predictive prophecy in the Bible? Extremely so. Scholars estimate that approximately one-fourth of the Bible is prophetic in nature. Prophetic statements found in the Bible number in the hundreds, and many of those prophecies have been fulfilled. This includes 333 prophecies that were fulfilled in the first coming of Christ. In these 333 texts, 451 details are delineated about the life of Christ.[12]

How significant is this? There are twenty-six books that exist today, alongside the Bible, that claim to be divinely inspired writings. Please note, however, that with the exception of the Bible, predictive prophecy is glaringly absent in all of those writings. There is no example of predictive prophecy in any of the other books that claim to be divinely inspired. For example, it is not found, anywhere, in the writings of Buddha, Lao-Tze, or Confucius.[13]

Keeping in mind the insane probability of getting the NCAA bracket 100 percent right, consider the mathematical probability (not the gambling odds) of a person fulfilling specific predictions made about the details of their life centuries before they appeared on Earth. Try to understand the astronomical probability of a single person (Jesus) fulfilling just eight of those prophecies! That is a mere two-and-one-half percent of the 333 prophetic texts. Well, the odds of one person fulfilling even that small amount of prophecies are the same as a blindfolded person picking a specially marked silver dollar out of a pile of silver dollars roughly the size of the entire state of Texas filled to a depth of two feet. That is one chance in *one hundred million billion.*[14] Such are the odds that a person could fulfill just eight (2.5 percent) of these 333 prophesies. That number is millions of times greater than the total number of people who have ever walked this planet![15]

The odds get even higher. What is the probability of fulfilling 48 (just 14 percent) of the Messiah prophesies? The probability has been computed at "one chance in a trillion, trillion, trillion, trillion, trillion, trillion, trillion, trillion, trillion, trillion, trillion, trillion!" (Stoner, *Science Speaks,* p. 105, cited in *The Case for Christ*, p. 199). Here is how to picture this: instead of a silver dollar, select a much smaller object, an electron. Suppose that one electron is marked and then thoroughly stirred into an entire mass of electrons, a mass much larger than the state of Texas, and then asking a blindfolded man to find the right one. Such is the probability of one person fulfilling 48 (14 percent) of the 333 messianic prophecies.

Trying to wrap your head around that reality causes the human mind to reel so fast that it spirals into a complete shutdown. It points to the divine mind that is behind the Bible, the intellect who loaded its content with specific predictions of future events with amazing accuracy. The supernatural evidence is persuasive that the Bible is what it claims to be, the Word of God.

CONCLUSION

And so, after assembling and logically organizing relevant evidence into a logical framework, the verdict in the field of predictive prophecy in the case for the trustworthiness of the Bible is in: the supernatural nature of the Bible can only be attributed to the existence of an all-knowing divine intellect whom the Bible refers to as God.

Pondering the full scope of all this evidence stretches the human mind beyond exhausting limits, so consider a brief story that will give your tired mind a rest by appealing to imagination. During the 1800s there was a Jewish man by the name of Simon Greenleaf. He possessed one of the greatest legal minds of all time and was an expert in the field of evidence. Greenleaf is regarded by some as the greatest authority on the trustworthiness of evidence who ever lived. He wrote three books that delineated guidelines on what constitutes evidence permissible in a court of law. His writings are still utilized as textbooks in law school educational curricula.

Greenleaf had one primary guiding principle: "Never make up your mind about any significant matter without first considering the evidence."[16] Because of his Jewish persuasion, he did not believe in Jesus Christ, much less in a resurrection from the dead, and he often mocked those who did. One day, in one of his classes, a bold student spoke up: "Professor Greenleaf, do you believe in the resurrection of Jesus?" Greenleaf answered that he did not. The student responded with a follow-up question: "But professor, have you considered the evidence?" For Greenleaf, that second question stopped time. He was completely stunned by the force of the query. It hit him with the hard, personal reality that, since he had never considered the evidence, he was in violation of his own sacred guideline in regards to his skepticism toward Jesus' resurrection.

Being a man of integrity, he committed himself to examine the evidence for the resurrection of Jesus. He did an exhaustive examination of every shred of evidence that he could possibly find and, when he finished the investigation, he put his conclusion in a book called *The Testimony of the Evangelists.* Here was his verdict:

> If the evidence for Christ's resurrection was presented to any unbiased jury in the world, they would have to conclude that Jesus rose from the dead.

This skeptical Jew became a believing Christian, and he went on to become a staunch defender of the Christian faith. This expert in what constitutes legitimate legal evidence reached a shocking overall conclusion: Christianity is, in fact, the only evidential historical religion in the world, and the Christian faith rests upon sound evidence that is so overwhelming and compelling that any honest person examining it with an open mind would, like himself, be irresistibly and inescapably drawn to it.[17]

The following story is told of an exchange that occurred between men of the sea. The captain of a ship looked out into a dark night and saw faint lights in the distance. Immediately he told his signalman to send a message: "Alter your course 10 degrees south." Promptly a return message was received: "Alter your course 10 degrees north." The captain was angered; his command had been ignored. So he sent a second message: "Alter your course 10 degrees south—I am the captain." Soon another message was received: "Alter your course 10 degrees north—I am seaman third class Jones." Immediately, the captain sent a third message, well aware of the fear it would evoke: "Alter your course ten degrees south—I am a battleship." Then came the reply: "Alter your course ten degrees north—I am a lighthouse." Notice that this tense confrontation ended immediately when the captain realized that the lighthouse specifically existed for his safety, and its message spoke with the firm voice of protective authority.

This is how the Bible was once viewed in American culture.

Dietrich Bonhoeffer, a German theologian who was hanged by the German army just two weeks before the end of World War II because of his support for a Hitler assassination conspiracy, once said, "The eternal law of God takes fearful vengeance when it is attacked or distorted." Little does our Western culture realize the danger it has exposed itself to by embracing a skeptical view of the Bible. Like an immature toddler who refuses to hold the hand of a protective parent while crossing a busy intersection, skepticism amounts to slapping away the hand of a God who is there to protect the slapper.

But now, unfortunately, as I mentioned earlier in this chapter, the Bible is the most criticized and least understood book in existence. However, once the literary, scientific, archaeological, and prophetic evidence in favor of the trustworthiness of the Bible is fully considered, it becomes obvious that much of the criticism is unfounded and unfair. The Word of God given to us through the Bible reveals a sweet story of love that emphasizes that there is a God, he wants a relationship with us, and he will meet us where we are—as people in need a savior.

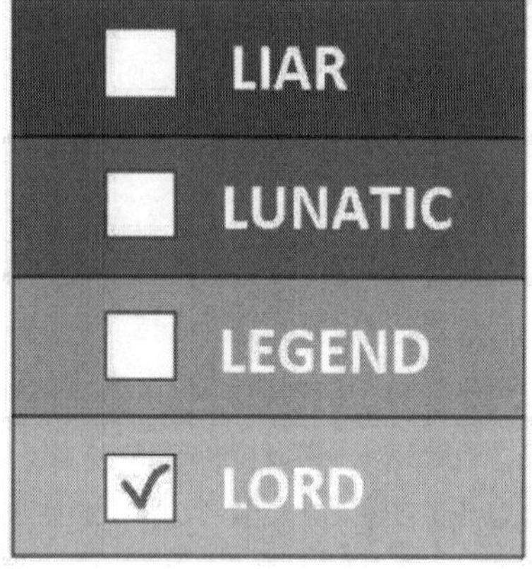

This chapter will conclude with the mention of four theories about who Jesus is. One: he was a *liar*, which means he was not telling the truth, and he therefore cannot be trusted. Second, he was a lunatic, which means he thought he was God, was not, and therefore should have been pitied, not trusted. Three: he is a legend, and never existed, so any thought of him needs to be disregarded. However, if the Bible is to be believed, and the evidence shows that it should, Jesus was not a liar, lunatic, or legend. He is Lord. A verdict has been established.[18] He is who he claims to be. Think of it in this way: if Jesus is a liar, lunatic, or mere legend, his word is not trustworthy, and anyone who listens to him would be a fool. But if he is Lord, then his word is trustworthy, and anyone who does *not* listen to him would be a fool.

PERSONAL STORY: RON

Hello. My name is Ron, and this is my story.

People say that you come to a fork in your road, and you either pick the right or the left, and I have had like four of them at different points in my life, and I just went everywhere but the right one.

I was born in Cincinnati, Ohio, in 1937. I left home when I was 17, and I just got into the devil's world, per se, and I spent twenty-four years in the US Navy. From what I remember while being in the service, we only had one chaplain. He did all the sermons for all of the different faiths on board the ship—everything from Jewish to Christian, really; whatever you wanted. But then the same chaplain would leave the ship and go off on binges while giving everyone the impression that he was out doing his job of seeing somebody in the local church or doing ministry duties elsewhere. But when he'd come back drunk, we all knew something was wrong with that picture.

I became disillusioned by his inconsistent behavior and lost faith in what he was supposed to represent. I just couldn't believe what he served up to us on Sunday when he would go out and drink and carry on during the week. I would go out and get drunk, you know, and run around and just come back without even knowing where I was, or knowing nearly anything at all; it was miraculous I could even find my way back onto the ship. I wasn't comfortable with my choices, either, but because of his hypocrisy, I couldn't talk to this phony chaplain, and I had no one else to talk to about my problems.

I got out of the service in 1979, but I still drank and carried on. My wife tolerated that for the most part, but then she'd be angry with me at times. Sadly, in 2009, I lost her to cancer. After my wife died, I was pretty upset and angry because I lost her so painfully after we had been together for forty-seven years. Once she died, I just didn't care about life. I became despondent, not wanting to do anything with my life.

One day I was in a fast-food drive-through line, and I said something derogatory to the person at the window, and my daughter, who was in the car with me, started crying. I snapped at her: "Hey, what's your problem?" She replied, sadly, "I just want my daddy back." So I said to myself: *There's something wrong somewhere here.*

Much later, while I was in an assisted living facility, I met a health coach named Cathy. I was in pretty poor physical condition, about 100 pounds overweight, and on a lot of different medications. We had some conversations, and I listened to what she had to say since she was trying to help me. At that point, I think I had just kind of given up on life.

She asked me one day if I'd like to go to church with her. And I said, "Where do you go?" She said, "The Church of The Apostles." They were having a January Guest Month, and she invited me to be her guest on one of the Sundays. They also offered a short course called Christianity Examined on how to have a personal relationship with the Lord. I decided to take the course.

On the first evening that we gathered, I announced that I was agnostic. The table discussion leaders did very well in listening to my skeptical questions and helping me finally get some meaningful answers.

During the course they gave us this little brown booklet and asked us to read one chapter a night while taking the course. Inside the book was the gospel of John, and as I began reading it I was overwhelmed with the way John described Christ: as being *the light of the world.* And then it says that Jesus invites us to receive his salvation but warns us too. It says in John 3:36, "He whoever believes in the Son has eternal life, but whoever rejects the Son will not see life, for God's wrath remains on him."

I thought that was great. So, yeah, when I did finish reading the gospel of John, I went outside and was sitting out in front of the facility. I just started crying, and as I was crying, I was praying to God asking Him to come into my heart and save me. I had the little prayer in the back of the booklet in front of me; I think it is called the sinner's prayer. They say you can say it in your own words if you prefer, so that's what I did. I just let all pent-up emotion and frustration that I had bottled up through the years burst out of me for about an hour.

Later that week, Cathy and I were driving to church for the final night of the course, and I looked at her and said, "Well, I just poured my heart out to the Lord like two nights ago, and you know that booklet that they gave us on the book of John? I said that prayer at the end of the booklet." And she said, "What?" And I said, "Yeah, you know, they have that prayer at the end of the booklet, and it's like a sinner's prayer. Well, I said it to God, and I even signed it on the line at the bottom of the page." She had a very shocked but satisfied look on her face, which was lit up in a happy way.

I spent years in darkness, thought I was happy, and did a lot of crazy things. But then when I found Christ, it was an entirely different sight. You just see things in different ways. So, like wearing your first pair of glasses, when you look out and see the world, it's entirely different. I feel lighter as a person. I feel no anger. I haven't been angry with anybody since that night . . . actually, since I poured my heart out to the Lord.

In reflecting back, Cathy tells me that she could really see the Lord working, step by step, in spite of me, and that he obviously had a plan for me that has a beautiful ending.

I now love coming to The Church of The Apostles. People want to know you, shake your hand, and welcome you into their church life. This is why I want to be here and stay here and be active in this church, which is very alive. Jesus Christ is the way, the only way you can come to God. He is the Savior. This is what I believe.

Small Group Interaction

REFLECTION QUESTIONS

- What objection do you hear most often against the Bible's trustworthiness?
- What part of this presentation on the reliability of Jesus' word caught your attention (made the deepest impression, struck you the most)?
- Did you have any thoughts or questions about the reliability of Jesus' word?
- What impact or relevance does the reliability of Jesus' word have on your spiritual journey?
- In general, do you think that the high level of criticism of the Bible is justified?

Next, Session 3: The Greatest Gift--The Good News of His Gospel

THREE

The Greatest Gift: The Good News of His Gospel

Little Zachary was doing very badly in math. His parents had tried everything: flash cards, tutors, mentors, special learning centers—everything they could think of to help his math. Finally, in a last-ditch effort, they took Zachary and enrolled him in the private religious school close to their home. After the first day, little Zachary came home with a serious look on his face. He did not even kiss his mother hello when he came through the door.

Instead he went straight to his room, and he started studying. Books and papers were spread out all over the room, and little Zachary was hard at work. His mother was amazed. She called him down to dinner. To her shock, the minute he was done, he marched back up to his room without a word and, in no time, he was back hitting the books as hard as before.

This went on for some time, day after day, while the mother tried to understand what was making the difference. Finally, Zachary brought home his report card. He quietly laid it on the table, went up to his room, and hit the books. With great trepidation, his mom looked at it, and to her great surprise, Zachary had gotten an A in math. She could hold her curiosity no longer. She marched up to his room and said, "Son, what is it? Is it the teachers?" Zachary looked at her and shook his head no. "Well then, was it the books? The discipline? The structure? The uniforms? What is it?" Little Zachary looked at her and said, "Well, on the first day of school, when I saw that guy nailed to the plus sign, I knew they weren't fooling around."

There is a serious moral to this funny story, and it is relevant to this presentation.

What is the real meaning of the cross? In chapter one, we talked about the uniqueness of Jesus and the three foundational principles that contribute to this distinction. The first: Jesus is the only religious founder who not only pointed to an ideal of perfection but *was* the ideal of perfection. He was God. Second, Jesus is the only founder of a religion who posed, not only as a *model* of what he taught, but as the *savior* of those he taught. And third, Jesus is the only religious leader who prescribed salvation through *self-abandonment* instead of self-improvement. These three pillar insights are woven throughout this book, and the focus of this chapter is on the second reality: Jesus is the savior of those who follow Him.

The second chapter surveyed supportive evidence for the reliability of the Bible to counter and balance the intense skepticism often leveled against it. Rarely are both sides of the debate presented fairly; it seems the case against the Bible gets the most press the most often.

As stated earlier, Christianity is:

"The *greatest* PERSON
with the *greatest* gift
of the *greatest* benefit
to the *greatest number* of people
through the *greatest* offer."

Our focus now turns to "the greatest gift." As with this chapter title, what is the good news of the "gospel"? This is actually a redundant statement—also what can be called a tautology—which occurs when the same idea is expressed twice but in different words. The word *gospel* itself means "good news." So the statement "the good news of the gospel" is like saying "the good news of the good news." Either way, the question is: *What is the good news?* Or: *What is the gospel?* To best answer the question, consideration needs to be given to two related insights: first, it has been rightly observed that religion is man's efforts to get to God, but that Christianity is God's effort to get to man. Second, the centerpiece of Jesus' mission on earth was not his life, but his *death*.

As we said previously, Jesus posed as the savior of those he taught. It's helpful to note that "the good news of the gospel" is found in the name of Jesus Christ. The name *Jesus* means savior, and the word *Christ* means anointed one. Both identify Jesus as the Messiah, the promised deliverer who came to save his people. So the name Jesus Christ is meant to designate Jesus as the "savior Messiah." The name Jesus, or savior, refers to his mission, and the name Christ, or Messiah, refers to his identity. After centuries of anticipation prompted by God's prophets foretelling the future, the promised Messiah had finally appeared on the scene of human history.

At the beginning of his public ministry, the savior-Messiah began to issue this proclamation to the world: "The time is fulfilled, the kingdom of God is at hand; repent and believe in the gospel" (Mark chapter 1 in the New Testament). Notice Jesus' threefold reference to: a new era, the nearness of the kingdom of God, and belief in the gospel. To paraphrase, Jesus was ushering in a new order in which the gospel is the gateway to the kingdom of God. In other words, the gospel is the key that unlocks the door into the kingdom of Heaven. It goes without saying that a clear understanding of the gospel is essential to any person who is serious about getting into the heavenly kingdom.

A first step toward understanding the word *gospel* will be a simple acrostic. There are six letters in the word itself: G-O-S-P-E-L. The gospel belongs to God, so the letter G refers to *God*; the letter O refers to the word *offered*; S stands for *Son*; P represents the word *payment*; the letter E stands for the word *eliminate*; and finally, the L stands for the word *life*. According to this acrostic, the word *gospel* looks like this.

The Gospel

God lovingly
Offered the sacrifice of His
Son as
Payment (or ranson) to
Eliminate sin and death and to replace it with
Life abundant and eternal!

Expanding the six single words to form a complete sentence reads like this: God lovingly Offered the sacrifice of his Son as Payment for our sins to Eliminate sin's effect on us and to replace it with Life abundant and eternal. That is the good news of the gospel. A single verse in the New Testament (John 3:16) captures it so well: "For God so loved the world that he gave His only begotten son that whoever believes in Him will not perish but have eternal life."

Keep in mind, the gospel does not emphasize Jesus in terms of a "teacher"; the gospel does not emphasize Jesus in terms of a "leader"; the gospel does not even emphasize Jesus in terms of a "preacher"; instead, the gospel emphasizes Jesus in terms of a *savior*, which was his primary reason in coming to earth. Here is the bottom line: *the core of Christianity is Jesus Christ.* And the core of Jesus' mission on earth was not his life but his death. All other religious founders aspired to live a model life that would inspire their followers to reach for an ideal of spiritual health and well-being. Their focus was on living a life that was worth emulating. Though Jesus did live a completely inspiring life, that was not the singular focus of his mission. When Jesus came to earth, the focus of his life mission was not his life but his death and resurrection. First Corinthians 15:3, 4 (in the New Testament) summarily states, "For I handed down to you as of first importance what I also received, that Christ died for our sins according to the Scriptures, and that He was buried, and that He was raised on the third day according to the Scriptures . . . "

It is helpful to note two ironies about the death of Jesus. The first is the age at which he died. Other major religious founders died at mature ages. Abraham (Judaism) died at age 175;

Buddha (Buddhism) died at the age of 80; Confucius (Confucianism) died at 70; Mohammad (Islam) died at 63; and Lao-tzu (Taoism) allegedly disappeared around the age of 40. But Jesus died an untimely death at the approximate age of 33—in the prime of his manhood. Second, Jesus would not only die a seemingly premature death, he was also brutally executed in the most cruel and humiliating way known in his day. While in most cases other religious founders died of natural causes, Jesus was condemned to die by execution through crucifixion.

But Jesus died an untimely death at the approximate age of 33—in the prime of his manhood.

In the last session, consideration was given to a variety of evidence in the case for the trustworthiness of the Bible, some of which could be debated since there are different ways to view evidence. But the fact of Jesus' death—and death by crucifixion—really is not a matter of debate but of undisputed historical fact. Consider this quote from a first-century historian, a Jewish man by the name of Josephus, who finished his first century history, *Antiquities of Jews,* in AD 93. A striking reference to Jesus is mentioned in his writings: *"At the time of Pilate, there was a wise man who was called Jesus. His conduct was good, and he was known to be virtuous. And many people from among the Jews and other nations became his disciples. Pilate condemned him to be crucified and to die, but those who had become his disciples did not abandon his discipleship. They reported that he had appeared to them three days after his crucifixion, and that he was alive. Accordingly, he was perhaps a messiah, concerning whom the Prophets have recounted wonders"* (Josephus, The Antiquities, 18:63-64.) Notice that in this first century statement, the writer recounts that there was an historical figure named Jesus, that this man Jesus was condemned by Pilate to die, and that he was executed by crucifixion. Josephus's statement is found as an extra-biblical source and confirms Jesus' crucifixion as an historical event.

Today, the most recognizable symbol of Christianity is the cross. Christians commonly wear crosses around their necks, on bracelets, and even hang them from the rearview mirror in their cars. When driving in cities and through the countryside, it seems there is a church on every corner and around every bend. Looking closely at all these church buildings, one can't help but notice that, often, at the most elevated point on those structures, are spires or steeples with the symbol of the cross resting at the top.

Today, the most recognizable symbol of Christianity is the cross.

Since the cross symbolized the most horrifying death of that day, why does the cross merit such an honored place in Christendom? Execution by crucifixion was engineered to inflict maximum pain upon its victims and yet stop just short of causing the victim to slip into unconsciousness—thus losing contact with their physical and emotional pain—or even to die. In other words, the aim was to inflict as much pain as possible while keeping the victim conscious, forcing them to experience the pain in this most hideous, unmerciful way. History tells us that some people hung on a cross for as long as a week before succumbing to death. And so the idea of the cross being a symbol that is cherished by Christians actually seems quite . . . mysterious. What would you think of a person who wore a necklace with a little electric chair dangling from it? Or a guillotine? Wouldn't that appear repulsive, almost sadistic? Yet the cross is still the primary recognizable symbol of the Christian faith.

Why do Christians focus so much attention on this cross when it represents such unimaginable pain, unspeakable horror, and traumatic humiliation to the person Christians hold in such high regard? The explanation for this seemingly irrational devotion lies in the true meaning of the cross. This devotion is not to the cross itself but to its profound meaning. *The cross itself is just an old, rugged piece of wood, but the meaning of the cross is a beautiful portrait of sacrificial love.*

The way Jesus' life ended was not simply a horrible misfortune caused by a riotous group of troublemakers whose misguided intentions got out of control and caused an unfortunate disaster. *Jesus approached his death with full intentionality.* He did not die by accident or natural causes. Jesus approached death with loving resolve, unflinchingly facing the prospect of his death, knowing full well the horrific nature of the death he was about to endure.

Notice the way Jesus spoke of his death. He said, "I did not come to be served, but to give my life as a ransom for many." That is probably the clearest statement that can be found in the Bible as to his mission. Again, Jesus says in John, chapter 10, "I am the good shepherd. The good shepherd lays down his life for the sheep." In John 15, in the upper room discourse between Jesus and his disciples on the night before his crucifixion, he said, "No man has greater love than this, that he lay down his life for his friends." Apparently, the disciples got that message of his self-sacrifice and wove it prominently into the fabric of the New Testament. In First Timothy chapter 2, it says, "There's one God and one mediator between God and men; the man, Christ Jesus, who gave himself as a ransom for all.

In John's gospel, one of the most familiar verses (3:16) begins with the sublime words, *"God so loved the world that he gave his only son . . ."* And in John's first letter, written to Christians, less familiar, but similar, words are found (3:16) which reinforce Jesus' sacrificial love as motivation to go to the cross: "We know love by this; that he laid down his life for us." And then, in Romans (chapter 5), the apostle Paul repeats the refrain: "God demonstrates his love toward us, in that while we were yet sinners, Christ died for us."

So while his death took many of his followers by surprise and was completely unimaginable to those who understood his goodness, it did not take Jesus by surprise. When it appeared that Jesus was defeated and being run out of Jerusalem, He was triumphantly leading the parade. He predicted his rejection, predicted that it would lead to his death, and specified even further that he would die by crucifixion.

THE TRUE MEANING OF THE CROSS

Now for a deeper dive into the true meaning of the cross—and this is where the enlightening value of the Bible asserts itself as it hands us the key that unlocks the mystery of this ancient symbol.

First, a helpful analogy. Keys are made with a series of pointed teeth and notches on the blade, and these are called bittings (rhymes with fittings). Teeth are the protrusions, and notches are the indentations on the blade of a key. Together, these two aspects of the key determine how it interacts with the tumblers inside the lock. If the bittings on the key match the tumblers inside the lock, the key successfully opens, or "picks," the lock. In essence, a code of sorts is formed on the blade of the key.

I would suggest that the key that unlocks the mystery of the cross has multiple teeth. The Bible relates certain key words that symbolize the teeth on a key. These words, when grouped together like teeth, like notches on a key, form a code that matches the mystery of the meaning of the cross.

First, a warning that these are big words, what my mother used to call "50-cent words," words not usually a part of everyday vocabulary. But as will be seen shortly, the profound meanings of these words are well worth the effort to understand them.

The first word is *propitiation* (hard to pronounce, much less understand). This word refers to "satisfying the demands of a wrathful deity through sacrifice." And yet this idea was not only understood but even *practiced* by other first century religions. The sense that it is used in Christianity refers to the satisfaction of God's demand for justice to appease his wrath toward human sin. Through Jesus' brutal death on the cross, he satisfied God's demand for justice and appeased God's wrath regarding the sin of man—our sin.

Through Jesus' brutal death on the cross, he satisfied God's demand for justice and appeased God's wrath regarding the sin of man—our sin.

The next word, closely associated with propitiation, is *atonement*. This word means "to cover by making amends for wrongdoing." By Jesus offering his life as a propitiation and satisfying the demand of God's wrath for our sin, he atoned for our wrongdoings. By Jesus dying in our place for our sins and wrongdoings, he covered them. It is interesting that when the English word atonement is hyphenated, it reads like this: *at-one-ment*. Is the nuance obvious? It implies a bringing together, a oneness, between previously alienated people by covering the offense that fractured the relationship.

The "at-one-ment" idea points to the third big word: *reconciliation*. Reconciliation means "to bring harmony between adversarial parties." The Bible speaks of the death of Christ being central to the work of reconciliation. In other words, when Jesus hung on the cross, suspended between Heaven and earth, representing God in Heaven and man on earth, Jesus reconciled, or brought together, these two adversarial parties.

So Jesus' death is the fulcrum that the lever of reconciliation rests upon as it tips God's response to sinners from the unfavorable side of the spectrum to . . . the *favorable.* Thus, the door to peace between a holy God and unholy sinners is now open.

The fourth word is *redemption*, and this means "to rescue" or "to buy back through a ransom payment." In the Christian sense of the word, it refers to the death of Jesus as the ransom price before God for all human wrongdoings. Jesus redeems, or liberates, people out of their bondage to sin and elevates them to a new and better place where they can experience freedom from sin and be at peace with God.

So, coalescing the impact of *propitiation, atonement, reconciliation*, and *redemption* into a unified whole brings about a most desirable effect, which is conveyed in the fifth and final word: *salvation.* This cluster of realities brings about salvation to those who embrace Jesus as their savior and position themselves as beneficiaries of the substitutionary death of Christ on the cross. Jesus' death, then, as interpreted by Scripture, was a sacrificial act of self-substitution, one in which he lovingly died

So, coalescing the impact of *propitiation, atonement, reconciliation,* and *redemption* into a unified whole brings about a most desirable effect, which is conveyed in the fifth and final word: *salvation.*

in our place to deliver us from God's wrath, grace us with a status of forgiveness, and set us free from the oppression of sin.

So, then, what is the meaning of the cross? The simple answer is that Jesus died because he was on a rescue mission. The Bible says that Jesus went to the cross, with love for man in his heart, and endured the horrors of crucifixion in joyful anticipation of the benefits that would come to those who believe in Him. This is why believers continually find themselves pondering a question that is set to music in the classic hymn "And Can It Be?": "Amazing love! How can it be that Thou, my God, would die for me?" In conclusion, *propitiation, atonement, reconciliation,* and *redemption* are the teeth on the key blade that match the code to the lock on the door that leads to *salvation.*

Key to Salvation

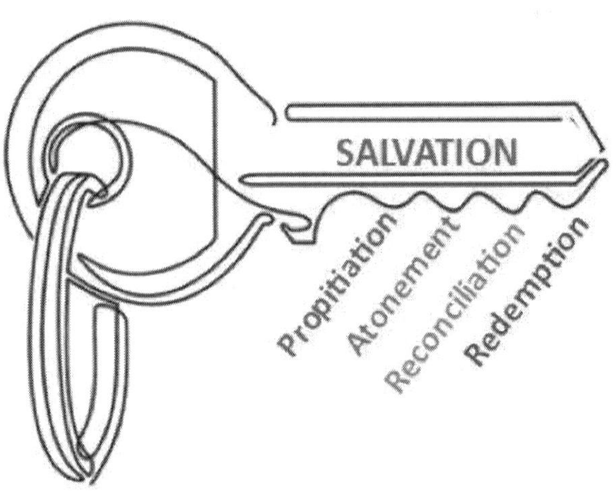

In Arlington National Cemetery in Virginia, there is a gravestone with a simple epitaph. It says: "I want to stand where you're standing." Underneath those words is the lovingly engraved story of an incident that occurred during the American Civil War. A Yankee soldier, only 19 years old, was part of a firing squad, assigned to execute a man for treason. As he closed one eye and took aim down the barrel of his gun, he was horrified to see that he knew the man he was about to shoot. He lowered his gun, walked over to his captain, and said, "I can't do it. That man has a wife and children at home. If I shoot him, I will not only end his life, but I will end their lives too. I will make his wife a widow, and I'll be robbing the children of their father. I can't do this." After a short discussion, they came up with the following plan. They agreed that the young soldier would take his condemned friend's place. The nineteen-year-old Yankee marched up to the (now) Confederate, the captive, and simply said, "I want to stand where you're standing." The captive took off his blindfold and walked away a free man, back to his wife and family, having received his life returned to him as a gift. But his freedom to go on with his life came at a great cost to another: the young man who had willingly chosen to die in his place. This is a perfect depiction of Jesus' willingness to die for his adversaries—us—because he considered their welfare more valuable than his life.

One of the most common beliefs in our culture today is that there are many paths to God. This comment is worth deconstructing. The word *path*, when used in a religious sense, is usually meant to refer to a set of ethics, a group of steps, or a list of dos and don'ts. Assuming that to be the meaning, then it needs to be clarified that there are *no paths to God.* The reason for this is that all paths share this assumption: personal goodness as the basis for a relationship with God. However, one of the most pride-shattering realizations that a person must come to grips with is that connection with God does not depend on personal performance. Now let's talk about why!

Though there are no paths to God, there is a *way* to God. In John 14:6, Jesus didn't say, "I am the path to God." On the contrary, he said, "I am the way to God." This is a subtle but significant distinction. Now to illustrate the point. Many religions teach a set of steps or a list of performance requirements that will eventually lead a person "to God." These suggestive pathways consist of a list of "dos." Here is a sampling of religions and a brief synopsis of their particular version of a path to God:

- **Animism** is found in primitive religions all over the world. The religion of animism teaches that there are higher deities who have turned people over to lesser deities or spirits, and that these lesser deities are mostly hostile toward human beings. So, to be spared the wrath of these lesser deities, people must behave, or these evil spirits will punish them harshly through disease, droughts, or death. So animism teaches its participants to behave according to the tribal codes of conduct to avoid the displeasure of the spirit world. Note the emphasis on "doing."
- **Hinduism** believes in *karma*. The law of karma has to do with good works as well as bad works. The better your karma, the belief goes, the better your chance of achieving freedom more quickly from the dreaded reincarna-

tion cycle. And by good karma, we experience extinction quicker through reincarnation. This is called *nirvana*, in which a person becomes one with the soul of the universe, which is Brahman. So the desired state of nirvana is reached by doing good karma, reaping what is sowed, and achieving oneness with Brahman as soon as possible. Note *again* the emphasis on "doing."

- **Buddhism**, another so-called "path to God," teaches enlightenment. And that means overcoming desire that causes you pain, and doing so through the noble eightfold path. This path is comprised of a list of "dos."
- **Islam** refers to the path to God being one of unquestioned obedience to an absolute deity.
- **Confucianism** teaches ethics, morals, dos and don'ts, and familial piety as a path to God.
- The **New Age** believes that God is within us and that divine energy is released from within, and this believed energy is the secret of happiness. New agers emphasize the immanence of God, whom they claim to be within us.

Keeping in mind that "religion is man's effort to get to God, while Christianity is God's effort to get to man," it can be rightly said that "Religion is spelled 'D-O'; Christianity is spelled 'D-O-N-E!'" Recapping these other paths to God:

- **Animism**: behave or the evil spirits will get you
- **Hinduism**: have good karma; experience extinction through reincarnation called nirvana
- **Buddhism**: enlightenment (overcoming desire that causes you pain)

- **Islam**: unquestioned obedience to an absolute authority
- **Confucianism**: ethics and morals
- **New Age**: divine energy released from within—this is the "secret" to happiness

By contrast, there is Jesus:

- **Jesus**: "It is finished!" or "It is done!" Jesus' final word on the cross just before he died—in Greek, *tetelestai*— is actually a commercial word which means "the debt is paid" (John 19:30).

Now, all of these religions claim to lay down paths to God, but if taken, sadly they won't lead to the promised destination. Any supposed pathway to God that is tied to a performance mindset of "dos and don'ts" or ethical maxims is not a true path to God. As stated earlier, while Jesus did not claim to be a path to God, he did claim to be *the way* to God. Jesus' way to God has nothing to do with performance but is based upon dependence. Religion is about us living a righteous life and offering it to God; Christianity is about Jesus living a righteous life and offering it for us.

You are probably wondering, "How can that possibly be true?" Here is how. If Jesus paid the debt, and paid it in full, that means there is nothing left for us "to do." If some kind person comes along and pays off your $20,000 credit card balance in an act of extraordinary kindness, would you continue to send in payments to your credit card company? In the same way, the foundation of our relationship with God is not what we do for him but what he has done for us.

I once heard a story that perfectly illustrated how Jesus is the way to God. On a clear day in a faraway land, the pilot of a small plane was flying over a jungle on his way to a village located in the general area. The plane developed engine difficulty and was going down, which forced the pilot to parachute out of the craft. Fortunately, he landed without injury in an open area that was cleared of jungle trees and foliage. Soon a local tribesman appeared and, in a language they both understood, offered to take the downed pilot to his intended destination. The pilot eagerly asked, "So, is there a path to the village?" The native replied, "No, there is not a path to the village, but there is a way." The pilot said, "Very good. Will you show me the way?" The native offered this profound response: "I am the way. You simply must follow me."

In the same sense that the way to the village was not a path, but a person, so the way to God is not a path, but a person. The pilot eventually reached safety, but not by his ability; instead, it came through his dependence on the ability of the guide. People reach eternal safety not through their own ability but through their dependence on the ability of Jesus.

The apostle Peter once said to Jesus, "Lord, you alone have the words of eternal life." And in Romans chapter 1, the apostle Paul says, "The gospel is the power of God unto salvation." This profound truth can be characterized in the following way. When it is said that Jesus, through his atoning death, became the source of eternal salvation, this is essentially what is meant:

- Jesus, the **perfect** person,
- offered the **perfect** sacrifice,
- and paid the penalty of our sin **perfectly**.

- In turn, he offers us a **perfect** forgiveness,
- gives us a **perfect** peace,
- dignifies us with a **perfect** love,
- promises to make each of us who believe in him a **perfect** person,
- and then, one day, to bring us to a **perfect** place.
- All of which makes Him the **perfect** savior.

Now, this idea of someone dying in our place—and that the favor of God is mediated to us through this person's death—is indeed a profound reality. Months ago, my wife and I, in a nearby coffee shop, had a conversation with a young lady who was studying for finals to achieve her master's degree. She was an accountant major, and I had great sympathy for her; accounting was one of my least favorite courses in college. Eventually, the conversation came around to the God-question. I said something to her like, "Well, if you died today, do you know if you would go to Heaven?" She said, "Good question, and I don't know the answer to it." So I said, "Well, if you did stand before God and he said, 'Why should I let you into Heaven?' what would you say?" And she said, "Well, I am religious, so I guess I would say, 'Because I've done the right things.'" I went on: "Would it surprise you if I told you that Heaven is not a wage, but a gift? You don't have to do anything to earn it. You just have to receive it." In an intense, shocked tone of voice, she said, "What did you just say?" I repeated, "Heaven is a gift. You don't have to do anything except receive it." She said, "In my entire religious life, no one has ever said that to me."

Then we explained how it could be true that Heaven is a gift, and this young woman became a Christian.

Six weeks later we caught up with her at a Starbucks coffee shop. Cindy and I are free spirits; we like to mix it up, you know? When we were seated, I asked our young friend, inquisitively, "So, tell me, now that God is in your life, what's it like?" Listen to her answer closely; I want you to grasp this. She said—and I quote her down to the very word—"Life is so different now when you wake up every morning knowing that a person loved you enough to die for you."

I marveled, silently, at her answer. She totally got it. She fully grasped the heart of the gospel. We had had absolutely no communication between those two meetings, so she didn't hear it from me. God alone had opened her eyes and heart to comprehend the gospel. So the good news of the gospel is that someone loved you enough, loved me enough, loved all of us enough, to die for us. The gospel truth is that Jesus, through his merit, has freed man from his futile efforts to try to earn the favor of God. He earned it for us.

I want to share an email I received from a participant in one of the first Christianity Examined courses we offered at our church in Atlanta:

> Dr J, I am a student in your Thursday night course. This has been a wonderful experience, and I believe it has been life-changing for me. When you spoke about the meaning and symbolism of the cross, well, I was thunderstruck. I have always considered the cross a rather gruesome symbol of a terrific murder and torture that was inflicted on a gentle soul and teacher. While you were talking, I kept an open mind and considered just

> what Jesus had given up if he were truly God. As you continued to explain his sacrifice, I began to think of just what his death could mean. Currently, my husband and I are trying to conceive, so I have "babies on the brain." I started to ponder what I would do if my child were ever in danger. There is no question that I would give my life for theirs. What if Jesus really did redeem his life for ours? And if he did barter his life for ours ad infinitum, then what greater love could a father have for his children than to die for us? So if he willingly went to his brutal and torturous death to save us all, then it was the greatest gift he could ever give. Then the cross could truly be a symbol of the eternal and limitless love that our father had for all of us. Dr J, for the first time in my life, I would like to wear a cross. Kind regards, Elisabeth."

All I could think then, and now, is to say: thanks for these precious reflections, Elisabeth. There is no way it could have been said better.

Since Jesus was a great teacher of parables, it would seem appropriate to finish this presentation of "the good news of the gospel" with a parable. Someone has said that the plight of sinful people is like a man in a vile, filthy pit, along with a huge serpent that he is trying to avoid. Man has fallen into a ghastly pit with a ghastly serpent. What happens now?

- Well, along comes an **animist**. He looks down into the pit and sees the serpent. His eyes open wide, and he flees back into the jungle, lest that same evil spirit heave *him* into the pit.

- Along comes a **Confucianist**, and he says, "Ah so, great man never falls in pit. But walk circumspectly and, henceforth, you will look where you walk." And he goes his way.
- The **Hindu** comes along and says, "Ah, my brother. You think you are in a great black pit, but that is the error of the mortal mind. The fact is that all is Brahman and Brahman is all, and this external world is merely an illusion. Therefore, the pit does not exist. Just think, therefore, there is no pit, there is no serpent, and all will be well. Peace."
- Along comes a **Muslim**, who sees the man down in the pit and says, "I will help you, my friend." And he reaches down and grabs him by the arm and pulls him halfway out of the pit, but then suddenly draws his knife and says, "However, you will become a Muslim, won't you?" "Oh, I could never do that," the man answers, and back into the pit he goes.
- Next comes the **Buddhist**, who looks down and says, "Dear friend, you are suffering greatly in the pit. And the reason that you are suffering is because you want to get out of this pit. It is your desire that is making you miserable. What you must come to is a cessation of all desires, and then you won't mind being in the pit."
- And then **Jesus** comes and looks with compassionate eyes upon the man in the pit. Into that foul and filthy pit he leaps! He assumes a protective stance between the man and the serpent. The monster serpent rears its ugly head, coils, and strikes at the savior, sinking its poisonous fangs into his side. As the deadly venom flows into the blood of

> Jesus, he lifts the man up and out of the pit. Jesus dies a miserable death, but the man finally goes free.

That, my friends, is a savior. That is the difference between Christianity and all other religions. And that is the good news of the gospel.

Small Group Interaction

PERSONAL STORY: APRIL

My name is April, and I am a sinner saved by the grace of God. Here is my story.

I was born in Austell, Georgia and have lived the majority of my life in Cobb County, though I have moved around a lot! I have a teenage daughter named Peyton. I am my mother's youngest child, my father's middle child, and I have three older brothers, one older sister, and one younger sister much closer to my age! Professionally, I work at an auto repair company, and I have been a member of The Church of the Apostles since 2019.

I grew up in a split family. My mother and father separated when I was a year old. I have a stepmother, Carol, who has been my stepmom almost my entire life. I lived full-time with my mom, and I visited my dad on weekends, holidays, and for vacations or just because. My relationships with my family were good for the most part, but there were a lot of dysfunctions as well that caused me a lot of damage.

I have amazing memories from my early childhood. One of my favorites is my mom singing songs to me like "You Are My

Sunshine" or "The Happiest Girl in the Whole USA" when she would wake me in the mornings. I now sing those same songs to my daughter when I wake her up. She made Christmas and birthdays absolutely amazing too! I also have so many happy childhood vacation memories with my dad, stepmom, and younger sister!

The problem was, however, that as much as my mom was amazing and fun and beautiful, she also was badly broken and profoundly scarred. She grew up in a dysfunctional family and had deep childhood wounds. She was in an extremely abusive thirteen-year marriage. As a single mom of four children, she struggled to make ends meet, working multiple jobs and struggling to pay utilities which would often get turned off. She would sometimes deprive me of essential things to fill her own selfish needs or to please a man because she desperately needed a man's love. I saw her with so many men that it caused me to develop a bad image of what sexual intimacy was meant to be. I never really felt 100 percent safe living with her because we moved so much, and I never got comfortable calling anywhere home. On top of that, we were often without one utility or another. I often switched schools in the middle of the year, so I had a harder time making friends. Also, I didn't have nice clothes, shoes, a house, or whatever that everyone else had, so I was teased. I never had any long-term friendships in my life—until now.

On the other hand, my dad was much more stable, and I yearned for that stability to feel safe. I couldn't live with him, though, because it would have hurt my mom too much! To hurt him, she would tell me that my dad never wanted me and that he wanted her to have an abortion after I was conceived.

The person she ended up hurting with those words, though, was me.

Around age ten or eleven, her verbal abuse started getting bad. It was around that time she was getting sick, but it took a while before she would finally get diagnosed with congestive heart failure. Almost all my influence growing up was from my mom's family, and the entire family are addicts. Some of them are functional, some not, and some are recovering or have been clean for years now. The family is full of generational sin that has led to these lives of addiction, poor mental health, and just a lifetime of struggle. At various times of my life I was also touched inappropriately by three different men in my family, and nothing was done about it. It was just basically dismissed. So, I was a suitcase packed full of damage with a ton of junk in my trunk.

I grew up knowing about God and Jesus, but it wasn't until many years later that I truly understood how vague my relationship with God was and how shallow the knowledge of my Christian faith was while growing up. I went to a Christian school my first couple of years of grade school, and my grandparents took me to Sunday School often. I memorized Bible verses and knew all the stories and songs. I loved to share them with everyone as a child. That was before I acquired all my damage and developed strong insecurities. Up until about my early twenties I was a good girl, prayed often, and had the basic belief that I was saved because I had asked Christ into my life, and that if I was "good" I would go to Heaven.

As I mentioned earlier, my mom got sick when I was about twelve, and after that, most days were bad, especially once she became addicted to pain medication. There were some rough times that led to me eventually going to live with my father just before I started high school. It was the most comfortable and stable three years of my childhood. I moved back in with my mom during my senior year of high school, and she passed away about eight months later.

Just after my mom died, I got my first apartment with my boyfriend, who would very soon be the father of my child. I graduated from high school two weeks after getting that first apartment and found out I was pregnant shortly afterward. I stayed busy to avoid grieving over my mom, and because I was so busy, I never had time to think about it. After a while this started to catch up with me; the pain became too much, and I started doing things completely out of character. It wasn't long before my daughter's father and I split up when she was about eleven months old.

Because taking pills was so common and accepted in my family, it was easy to get just about anyone to give me a Xanax when I wanted to take off the edge. This is where my addiction began.

During this time I started dating probably the worst person I could have at such a vulnerable time in my life. He was older than me, fun and exciting, and we started drinking and taking pills daily. He introduced me to a harder drug. It didn't take long for me to become addicted. Almost immediately, everything I had up until that point in my life I started to lose, little by little. Not only my home and material things but also everyone in my life I had been close to before.

I was working crazy hours and even sold my body for a brief time to support both of our habits while he rarely had a job. All the while he was mentally and physically abusing me and breaking me down to my absolute lowest self. My daughter had been taken away from me, and for one year I could only have supervised visits. I was at my absolute lowest, and I honestly wanted to die. But I'm not a suicidal person, so instead I just got high every day hoping it would take me out.

About a month after my daughter was taken, I got into a bad car wreck that I walked away from without a scratch. I don't know why, but that wreck opened my eyes to my dreadful condition. For some reason it made me realize that even though I had become this horrible person that even I was disgusted with, God had not given up on me. I finally decided to get clean, and I started to change my life. I got a new job at an IHOP restaurant about a month into my sobriety. There I met a girl who was openly lesbian. I pursued her and we began dating. Though I knew this romantic relationship was wrong, she represented a safe love in my life.

As I began making efforts to reactivate my faith and my relationship with God, it just wasn't sitting right with my soul being in a romantic relationship with a woman. I started searching the Bible for something, anything that gave me approval for this relationship. In my pursuit I started attending a Bible study with people I met at work. Once they found out I was in a relationship with a woman they made me feel awkward and uncomfortable, and they also devoted an entire Bible study to going over verses that condemned homosexuality. I felt their full condemnation—that was the last Bible study I did with them.

This was such a delicate time in my journey with Christ, but luckily God was still not giving up on me. My aunt Carol, who is a member at The Church of the Apostles, was persistent in trying to get me to church with her. She invited me to a Christianity Examined course led by the evangelism pastor. I really enjoyed what he taught, so I signed up for a one-on-one meeting with him. We talked about my situation, and his response and advice were different than anyone I had ever talked to before. He didn't tell me I was wrong or remind me of what the Bible says, and he didn't look at me like I was awful, as many people usually did. His attitude toward me never changed, and he told me, "April, I am not going to tell you to go home and make some huge, drastic decision. All I want you to do is continue to actively seek God and build a relationship with him, and also when you pray, ask Him to remove anything from your life that is not part of His plan." So much anxiety about this situation was lifted off my shoulders. Had he handled that any differently, I probably would have walked out of the church and never gone back. I started going to a follow-up Bible study, and as my relationship with God and my faith grew, God eventually removed the other woman from my life, and did so in the most delicate way, which was an answer to my prayer.

Through the follow-up Bible study, I learned about another church ministry called Living Waters. I had no idea the level of healing that would come from this ministry. Living Waters freed me of so much shame and regret and helped me heal so many deep childhood wounds. I learned what a real, authentic relationship with Christ was, and I learned to know and understand better when Christ is in communication with me. I developed amazing relationships and received so much love and prayer from complete strangers. They had no reason to love me, but they did anyway. Even after hearing all of my ugly secrets, they still loved me.

The part of Living Waters that impacted me most was understanding the mother wound. A lady named Jeanine gave her testimony one night and, at the end of it, tears were streaming down my face. So many wounds that I wasn't even conscious of anymore were resurfacing. That night was so extremely emotional for me, and I left there crying so hard I probably shouldn't have been driving. The next day I woke up feeling ten pounds lighter. I committed to finishing the class, and it helped heal my shame and guilt to a level that I cannot be anything but grateful for.

Though not perfect, my life is much better now. During the times when I think about the horrible things I did, I cringe and start to beat myself up again. I start letting the lies creep back into my mind. The truth is that though those things were and still are horrible, I have finally been able to forgive. I eventually accepted that I cannot change what I did in the past or make it go away, but I do have control over everything I do in my future. And now I have God leading the way.

The cross used to be just a symbol to me, a piece of jewelry, a sticker, to show that you are a Christian. Now the cross means so much more to me. The cross represents life and resurrecting power. If it weren't for God sacrificing his Son on that cross for my sin, I would be dead. One of my favorite Scriptures states, literally, what God did for my life: "He lifted me out of the slimy pit, out of the mud and mire: he set my feet on a rock and gave me a firm place to stand" (Psalm 40:2). Once I gained a clear knowledge of confession and repentance, how to listen to God, the power of forgiveness, and the power of prayer, I learned what an authentic and personal relationship with God looks like. I stay in constant communication with Jesus by reading some type of Christian material almost daily, whether it be the Bible or a devotional book. I spread my joy and my love for him with everyone.

I am working hard now on some goals and stepping out of my comfort zone to live a life through which, hopefully, I can serve him better and follow his calling for me. I do have days when I struggle, but my worst days now are better than my best days before he pulled me out of the muck!

Thank you for listening to my story! As you now see, I am a sinner saved by his wonderful grace mediated to me through his sacrificial death on the cross.

REFLECTION QUESTIONS

- Up until now, what did the word *gospel* mean to you?
- What part of this presentation on the "good news of the gospel" caught your attention (made the deepest impression, struck you the most)?
- Do you have any thoughts or questions about the "good news of the gospel"?
- What aspect of April's story was most meaningful to you?
- What impact would you say the "good news of the gospel" has on your journey? (What relevance does this topic have to your spiritual journey?)

Next, Session 4: The Greatest Benefit--The Transformational Power of Genuine Faith in Him

FOUR

The Greatest Benefit: His Transformational Power

Before beginning the fourth and final presentation, a brief recap of what has been covered is in order. In the first presentation, three insights were discussed that set Jesus apart from all other religious founders. First, Jesus is the only religious founder who not only pointed to an ideal of perfection, but *was* the ideal of perfection. Second, Jesus is the only founder of a major religion, one who posed not only as a *model* of what he taught, but as the *savior* of those he taught. And then, third, Jesus is the only religious leader who prescribes salvation through *self-abandonment* instead of self-improvement.

The second presentation covered extra-biblical evidence that confirmed the trustworthiness of the Bible, God's primary means of both revealing himself to us and clarifying the terms of a personal relationship with him.

The third presentation featured an in-depth reflection on the good news of the gospel. The person of Jesus is the core of Christianity, and the core of Jesus' mission on earth was not his life, but his death. His death is the key that unlocks and opens the door to a relationship with God.

Now, having presented the case for the uniqueness of Jesus, the trustworthiness of his word, and the good news of his gospel, it is time to connect the dots between these realities and their benefit to people who choose to follow him.

As stated earlier, Christianity is:

**"The *greatest PERSON*
with the *greatest gift*
of the *greatest benefit*
to the *greatest number* of people
through the *greatest offer.*"**

The fourth and final presentation will spotlight the transformational power of a genuine, authentic faith in him. Faith connects the above truths about Jesus to the human heart and releases his transformational power in a person's heart. Faith is the means through which a person "internalizes" the gospel, through which Jesus becomes personal, and once Jesus becomes personal, it's the relationship with him that makes life transformative!

We have discussed the proposition that the death of Christ is the heart of the gospel. Out of this proposition flows this question: "What is your heart response to the heart of the gospel?" To answer this question with clarity, there are a couple of related questions I would like to pose, and I urge you to respond privately.

The first question: *If you fall asleep tonight and wake up somewhere other than your bedroom, how sure are you that you will be in Heaven?* Where would you position yourself on the spectrum below that authentically reflects your confidence level that you are Heaven-bound?

0% sure ______________________________ **100% sure**

The second question: *If you are confident you are going to Heaven, exactly what are you basing the hope of your salvation on?*

__ *I tried my best to please him*

__ *I lived by the golden rule*

__ *I was baptized while I was in high school*

__ *I was a good person*

__ *I grew up in a Christian family*

__ *I never did anything really bad*

__ *I tried to love my neighbor as myself*

__ *I attended church faithfully*

__ *I loved and provided for my family as best I could*

__ *I memorized the Ten Commandments*

__ *Other*

By design, these questions enable a person to clarify the status of their relationship with God. Your answers to these questions identify your correct spiritual address, so to speak.

So what does it mean, exactly, to be saved? In a mock preacher voice, friends and I used to ask this question cynically back in my skeptical days, but the serious consequences of the question demand that it be approached in a more serious way. The idea of being saved is most often associated with being rescued from physical danger. But when used in the spiritual sense, there is a deeper meaning to the word "saved" that is rarely referenced, even in church circles.

While the word does include the idea of rescue from an outside danger, it can also be translated "to heal." And the reason we need to be rescued from the threat of external danger is because we exist with an internal brokenness. That brokenness resides deeply within us and creates a rupture in our relationship with God. Once the inner brokenness within us is healed and the inherent disconnect in our relationship with God fixed, that, in effect, removes the threat of an external danger. The core meaning of the word, therefore, need not be overlooked.

Now, if there is a need for healing, doesn't that also imply the presence of sickness? If sickness exists, shouldn't effort be made to identify the disease? Once the disease is identified, the next step is obviously to begin the search for a cure.

The first step in the healing process is to diagnose the disease. I grew up in a traditional religious background and attended a parochial religious school at which I was instructed thoroughly in the tenets of my childhood faith. There are certain things learned in childhood that aren't forgotten in adulthood. One of the most influential maxims I learned, one that profoundly affected the way I thought of myself, was this: to err is human, but to forgive is divine. This is to say that, by nature, I am prone to do the wrong thing.

Another parallel insight I learned about myself in my religious upbringing is that our hearts are naturally inclined toward evil. When I was a child, that was kind of a scary thought, but as I matured, I gradually realized that this was not alarmist hyperbole but rather a sobering statement of fact.

When I was a child, that was kind of a scary thought, but as I matured, I gradually realized that this was not alarmist hyperbole but rather a sobering statement of fact.

If you take your hand off the steering wheel when driving down the interstate, how long does the car continue to go straight? Not very long, and that is very dangerous living in a place like Atlanta. What happens very quickly is that the car, left to itself, begins to swerve dangerously to the right or left. That is a suitable analogy of the human heart. The tendency of the unrestrained human heart is to gravitate, naturally, toward evil.

The word *sin* means "to miss the mark" and is like shooting arrows at a target. When we aim for the bull's-eye of moral perfection, we often miss the mark. It's not that we don't aim for it; rather it's that, despite our best efforts, we just can't ever seem to hit it. Along with sin meaning "to miss the mark," the word also means "to fall short." Picture it this way: God is exalted in the heavens as the high ideal of perfection, and we are down below in the real world of imperfection. We try to reach up to God's level of perfection, but we fall short, as noted in Romans 3:23: *"For all have sinned and fall short of the glory of God."* The word *fall* is a present tense word signifying a current, ongoing reality. Put simply, our performance does not rise to his standard.

So the gap between God's ideal of perfection and the reality of our imperfection is called sin, and according to this verse and others, the problem of sin is universal. Notice the word "all" in each of the following verses in the Bible:

> "*For all have sinned . . .* " (Romans 3:23)
>
> "*All of us like sheep have gone astray . . .* " (Isaiah 53:6)
>
> "*For we all stumble in many ways . . .* " (James 3:2)

A book was written in the 1920s with the title *Whatever Became of Sin?*[19] The book opens with the story of a man standing on a busy street corner in Chicago dressed in very dark attire and wearing dark sunglasses. As he stands on that street corner, he points randomly at the people passing by, repeating in an ominous tone of voice the word "guilty." Considering the universal nature of sin, how could he miss?

The difficult reality is that sin flows naturally out of everyone's core. To regulate this harsh reality, the human tendency is to minimize and underestimate the gravity of our sin. As underestimating physical disease can be threatening to one's physical health, the same is true for our spiritual health. We do not realize that the nature of sin is like the makeup of an iceberg—between eighty and ninety percent of it lies below the surface of the water. How much sin lurks below the waterline in our hearts? Just how serious is the problem of sin?

Here is an effective way to dramatize the point. By your own estimation, how many sins do you commit in a single day? Would you say that three sins a day is a reasonable estimate?

Usually, I manage to do that before breakfast in the morning. I easily commit at least three sins minimum within a 24-hour period, which means that cumulatively, my sin total reaches at least a thousand sins a year. And that means that if I live out the normal life span, which would take me into my seventies, I'm going to stand before God with at least seventy thousand willfully committed sins. Wow! Consider this: how many sins does it take to keep me out of Heaven? How many violations of the law does it take for a person to get thrown in jail? *Just one.* I was thrown in jail twice while I was in high school, both times for a single offense: possession of alcohol in a dry county. James 2:10 (in the New Testament) says, "Whoever keeps the whole law and stumbles at one point is guilty of all."

God is perfect, and the only way people can get to Heaven is to be perfect. If it only takes one sin to disqualify you from Heaven, and knowing that you are going to stand at the gates of Heaven at the end of your life charged with at least seventy to eighty thousand sins, how do feel about your prospects? To what degree can you identify with this prayer?

> Dear God, so far today I have done all right. I have not gossiped or lost my temper, I have not cheated anyone out of money or stared at a beautiful woman in the wrong way. I have not been grumpy or selfish, and I am glad of that. I have not used any swear words, done anything really dumb, or acted in a way that embarrassed me or my family. I have not coveted anything that belongs to my wealthy next-door neighbor. But in a few minutes, Lord, I must get out of bed, and from then on, I'm going to need all the help I can get.

That prayer effectively makes the point that we do have an albatross around our necks, and it is called sin. The worst part about our sinful nature is the tendency to think that life is all about us. Stated humorously, sinful people by nature want to sit at the front of the bus, the back of the church, and be the center of attention. So, sin is the disease, and the good news of the gospel is that Jesus is the physician who can heal the disease. In the same way that those who are sick need a doctor, those who are sinners need a savior. You may still be thinking: *I just don't see the seriousness of my sinfulness.* Probably neither do you realize that you are sitting on a planet that is spinning around on its axis at approximately one thousand miles an hour and that this same planet is also hurtling through space at approximately sixty-seven thousand miles per hour. Some things in life are simply harder to comprehend than others—and so it is with our sin nature.

So being healed and being saved are similar in nature, one dealing with the body and the other dealing with the soul. However, in both situations, healing does not come without recognition of the disease. Disease recognition precedes healing application. As it is with the body, so it is with the soul. Martin Luther stated it best in the following words: "The recognition of sin is the beginning of salvation."

Years ago, an insightful follower of Jesus was asked by his local newspaper to write an essay on the question, "What's wrong with the world?" His entire response was as follows:

> Dear Sir,
>
> I am.
>
> Yours, G.K. Chesterton[20]

To assess your comprehension of your condition, please indicate where you would place yourself on the sinful awareness continuum.

What is your awareness level of your sinfulness?

0% sure ______________________________ **100% sure**

What motivates a person to spend money on medicine is the awareness that he or she is sick. The higher our awareness of our sinfulness, the more motivated we will be to seek help. Hopefully, you are motivated at least enough to keep reading beyond this bad news of our sinfulness to hear the good news of how Jesus can fix it.

The Bible speaks clearly to the question of how a person is saved, in Ephesians 2:8, and it reads like this: "By grace you are saved though faith." If there is a plainer statement in the Bible about how a person's fractured relationship with God can be reset, I'm not aware of it. Unpacking it is well worth the effort at this point.

Notice that it says "by grace" a person is "saved." Grace is a concept that is unique to the Christian faith and not found in other religions. Once, C.S. Lewis, a brilliant twentieth-century English philosopher, entered a room full of Oxford professors who were having a friendly debate over what makes Christianity unique. Upon being asked his opinion, Lewis replied, "Oh, that's easy. Grace."[21]

Grace defined means "God's unmerited favor extended to an unworthy subject."

Grace finds its origin in the sacrificial death of Jesus through which he gave himself to atone for the human problem of sin. God was so pleased by his death that it earned a vast, unlimited reservoir of favor that Jesus now makes available to those who come to him for healing in their fractured relationship with God. Some insightful person captured the essence of grace through the following acrostic:

God's **R**iches **A**t **C**hrist's **E**xpense!

Jesus merited this wonderful favor through his perfect work on the cross. Jesus earned it, and it is his to give freely to those who look to him.

Our acceptance by God does not depend upon what we have done for him, but upon our acceptance of what he has done for us.

The verse further expands the idea of salvation by grace by adding the word faith so that it now reads, "By grace you are saved through faith." The instrument that activates saving grace in a person's life is faith.

To best understand faith, it needs to be broken down into three simple pieces. The first component is **knowledge**. Knowledge involves the mind and affects our cognitive awareness of reality, or truth. Further, it should be noted that faith does not operate in a vacuum but always requires an object. So faith starts with knowledge, or awareness, of a proposed reality.

The second ingredient of faith is **assent**. Assent is a confirming response to a proposed reality that one believes is valid or true. In other words, when a person is made aware of a proposed truth or a reality, he or she will have an assessment reaction of what is now placed on their consciousness. Assent is synonymous with agreement. And if knowledge involves the mind, assent involves the emotions. The etymology of the word *emotion* involves nuances from three different languages. The French word *emouvoir* means "to stir up"; the Greek word *emotere* translates to "energy in motion"; and the Latin word *emovere* means "to shake" or "to stir." Together, these shades of meaning combine to define emotion as a deep, personal reaction. People have a capacity to react and assess reality, or the absence of it, which involves emotions, at least to some degree.

The third and final aspect of faith is **trust**. Trust is an elusive word but can be best understood to involve these aspects: *firm belief in*, *confidence about*, *reliance upon*, and *willingness to live by*. Yes, that's a mouthful, but all of these insights are necessary to do justice to the profound word *trust*. A combination of these yields this definition of trust: "confident belief that leads to continuous unwavering reliance."

The Scriptures say that a threefold cord is not easily broken, so weaving knowledge, assent, and trust together form a strong cord, or a bond of faith. I am of the opinion that as knowledge is a function of the mind, and as agreement involves the emotions, similarly, trust is linked to the will. Therefore, a healthy, vibrant faith necessitates that the mind, the emotions, and the will be in alignment, producing a total-person entrustment.

To better understand how these three components weave together to form true faith, let's now organize them into equations. The first scenario goes like this. In the deep South, where most people have at least a basic knowledge of God, knowledge is often equated with faith, which is to the detriment of many. What is the value of mere knowledge about God? James

2:19 (New Testament) says that "the demons believe and tremble."

This is detrimental because knowledge without assent and trust is actually a form of skepticism. This represents knowledge with no personal buy-in. In other words, this person is familiar with the idea of God but has never fully internalized the implications of this knowledge. Note that there are different types of skepticism. Passive skepticism is characterized by a general indifference. This person would say, "Okay, I know there is a God, but so what?" An active skeptic would say, "Many people believe in the idea of a supreme being, but I seriously doubt it." Their equation looks like this:

This is detrimental because knowledge without assent and trust is actually a form of skepticism.

Knowledge – Assent – Trust = Skepticism

Peanut butter is not equal to a peanut butter cookie. Peanut butter mixed with sugar and butter equals a peanut butter cookie. In the same way, knowledge does not equal faith. However, knowledge mixed with agreement and trust does.

The second scenario is a type of middle ground. This characterizes those who possess a general knowledge about God and have no conflicts with this knowledge. While this is a good start, it too falls short of true faith. Such people do church regularly, smile when God's name is mentioned, affirm gratitude toward God with others for daily blessings, give lip service about praying for sick relatives, and are careful not to use the Lord's name in vain when they get angry. However, when life goes south, they get "nervous and jerky." They believe that only an idiot drives the speed limit when late getting somewhere. They believe that God helps those who help themselves and are not above unethical behavior when large sums of money are at stake. In other words, though they believe in God, they ultimately put no trust in God. Though they would not dispute that God is all powerful, they hold all the personal power cards in their own hand and maintain complete control over their lives. They trust in themselves, not God, and live conflicted lives. When spelled out in an equation, their attitude toward God looks like this:

Knowledge + Assent – Trust = Ambivalence

The ambivalence results from a conflicted attitude toward God based upon a conditional reliance that causes a person to swing back and forth between trust and distrust, approach and avoidance, serenity and agitation. The ambivalent person only looks to God when they have no choice after having exhausted all other options within their control.

The third scenario is the "all-in" situation. The person in this position is hitting on all three cylinders of knowledge, assent, and trust, operating out of a fully internalized faith, with all their inner moving parts flowing in a cohesive direction. This person is in full agreement with the knowledge of God and trusts this God with full personal buy-in. As a result, transformational faith is in play, and

> Even when the winds of adversity blow, this authentic faith tranquilizes the atmosphere that surrounds this person.

there is heavenly peace in this person's corner of the universe. Even when the winds of adversity blow, this authentic faith tranquilizes the atmosphere that surrounds this person. They confidently say, in the face of hardship, "God is in charge, all is well." This is what true, healthy faith looks like:

Knowledge + Assent + Trust = Faith

Healthy faith manifests behavior that is consistent with a "confident belief that leads to continuous, unwavering reliance." An air of serenity flows out of one's core, enveloping the total person and the personal sphere they operate within. Trust is the activator of God's power in this person, and it has a linchpin effect of holding all the elements together. Thus, when trust breaks down, faith disintegrates into a weak imitation that is anemic and powerless. The trust "front" on the battlefield is where the battle is either won or lost in the struggle for genuine faith. Since the breakdown of faith almost always occurs in the trust aspect, it will be profitable to stop and drill down more deeply here. The most blessed of all people are those who get the trust component right in their experience with God.

At this point, a few relevant illustrations will be helpful.

- Nicky Gumble tells the following story in his book about the Alpha course. Years ago, a Scotsman decided to leave his home country and go to the South Hebrides Islands off the west coast of Scotland. He wanted to take the message of Christianity to a group of tribal people who were cannibals. Once he got there, he decided he would translate the Gospel of John into their native language. At this point, he encountered a major obstacle. In the context of these cannibalistic people, there was no equivalent word in their language for the word *trust*. Because of the savage culture, he had to overcome the barrier posed by a language which had no concept of trust, much less a word for it. So, as he was struggling to find an accurate way to communicate the idea of trust, here is how he stumbled onto it. One day, he was sitting in a chair, something like a bar stool, and as his servant walked in, he pulled his feet up off the floor and rested his entire weight on the chair. Then he looked at his servant and said, "Give me a word in your language that describes what I'm doing right now." And the servant spoke a word that adequately described what it meant to "put one's whole weight of reliance upon something." While resting his entire weight upon the chair, he was exercising confident belief that led to an unwavering reliance. He was demonstrating faith in the chair by leaning his entire weight on it. Using the servant's word, he instructed his listeners, in a whole new way, on the reality of faith in Jesus and successfully conveyed the concept of trust to an inherently distrustful culture. The word in their native tongue which meant "to lean upon or to put your whole weight upon" was the dynamic equivalent of trust, which paved the way for the native people to comprehend belief in God and faith in Jesus.[22]

The following is a fascinating illustration of true faith.

- Perhaps the life experiences of an acrobatic performer named Charles Blondin most strikingly illustrate the crucial role of trust in genuine faith. To say that this man could do amazing things on a tightrope under dangerous circumstances would be the understatement of the century. He is most famous for constructing a rope across Niagara River in 1859 and going back and forth, high above the roaring rapid waters, in occasional high winds while simultaneously doing amazing things. One day he put on a blindfold and walked all the way over to the other side and back. Other times, he got extremely creative when he crossed on stilts, pushed a wheelbarrow across, stood on a chair, and one time he actually stopped to read a newspaper. However, that is not the end of the story. One day, Blondin announced that he was going to cross Niagara with a man on his back. In front of the largest crowd to ever watch, Blondin announced the name of the person he was going to carry over, Harry Colcord his manager. Initially Colcord thought Blondin was joking but realized that he was serious. He hesitated at first but after thinking about it, based upon all that he had seen Blondin do so far, be agreed to go along with the decision.

In spite of the terrifying risks associated with such an idea, Colcord knew firsthand of Blondin's uncanny ability to do the impossible against death-defying odds. Based upon this firsthand knowledge of Blondin's expertise, he eventually assented to Blondin's ability to pull off such a feat, and trusted him with his life. In spite of struggling at certain points, they made it safely across. Blondin's manager not only had an objective belief in him, but he exercised a personal trust in Blondin.[23]

On the other hand, the risk-taking gesture of Blondin's mother's embodied what true faith is all about. To enter a genuine relationship with Jesus, one has to exercise a real faith in him that engages the mind, emotions, and will. His transformational power is released in the heart that is controlled by trust.

There is a verse in the book of Hebrews that dramatizes the essential nature of faith. Hebrews 4:2 says, "For indeed we have heard good news preached to us, just as they also did, but the word they heard did not profit them because it was not united by faith in those who heard." Notice how clear this verse is. It is saying that unless the good news, when heard, is united in a person's heart by faith—which involves knowledge, agreement, and trust—it is of no benefit to the hearer. So, by grace we are saved *through faith.*

Ephesians 2:8, 9 goes on to clarify the role of personal goodness and good works in the salvation experience. Personal goodness and good works are commonly cited by the vast majority of people as the basis for their hope of salvation—if they have one. However, what they are placing their hope in is direct conflict with the obvious intent of this verse. To those who go to sleep at night with a false assurance that their goodness and their good performance will secure for them a home in Heaven, the words of this text are a serious warning: "By grace you are saved by faith, that not of yourselves, not as a result of your works." This is the point where prideful human nature struggles to let go of its own efforts to resolve the disconnect between itself and God. Putting one's full weight upon Jesus and trusting in his atoning work means that a person must let go of any shred of trust in themselves that they can earn the favor of God.

As stated earlier, faith always requires an object, and it is no better than the object on which it is placed. I once read a story of two men floating down a river unwittingly headed straight for a deadly waterfall. On their being warned with shouts from the riverbank, one man jumped onto a log next to their boat and the other took hold of a rope thrown to him by some concerned onlookers on the bank. The man who grabbed the rope was pulled safely ashore, but the other drifted perilously on the log, over the waterfall, and was never heard from again. Both men had faith, but only one put his faith in an object that could save him, while the other put his faith in an object that could not.

People unwisely put their trust in their imperfect character and their imperfect efforts to try to attain an objective that requires perfection. This misplaced faith in imperfect human ability is futile. Jesus offered the perfect sacrifice that perfectly matched the demands of perfection, and faith in his rescue efforts will get us to safety. Faith in our imperfection, which will never match up with the required perfection, only leads to a perilous end. Jesus' efforts are the perfect solution, and there is no need to add our efforts to it—after all, how can anyone possibly hope to improve perfection? Saving faith involves reliance upon the right object, and in this case, the right object is Jesus' perfection, not our imperfection. Along these same lines, faith in faith itself is futile simply because faith must have an object. Faith is a connector that has no power in and of itself to do anything other than serve a connecting function between a subject and an object that has the power to act on behalf of the subject. Similar to a lamp and a plug, the lamp wire connects the two and allows electricity to flow from the electrical outlet to the lamp empowering it to give off light. In the same way that there is no power in the lamp wire, neither is there power in faith itself—they are both nothing more than connectors. Faith in Jesus empowers us to receive salvation.

Back to the role of good works in the salvation equation. It's important to put this truth in a realistic framework that will completely dispel any notion that a person can earn the favor of God. Suppose a great crowd gathers on the west coast of California, each person hoping to swim to Hawaii, roughly a twenty-three-hundred-mile journey. A whistle blows and the crowd jumps into the water and starts swimming from the shore. Some will not make it beyond deep water because not everyone knows how to swim. Casual swimmers will probably get a hundred yards or slightly more. Amateur swimmers will make it for about three or four hundred yards, maybe even a mile. Professionally well-trained swimmers may eventually get several miles from the shore. But no matter how far anyone gets from the California shore, relative to the destination in Hawaii, not one person will come even close, and in the end everyone who attempts this feat will drown.

Some use a comparison standard and reason, "Well, I haven't murdered anybody, I'm not a thief, and relatively speaking, I am a good person." But relative to what? Relative to the efforts of others, a person can falsely think they are better than most and stand a better chance of succeeding in their pursuit of eternal life. But sadly, relative to God's ultimate standard of perfection, none of us gets close. So, belief in the sufficiency of human ability to reach an acceptable level of moral perfection that merits God's favor must be abandoned completely. For its proper exercise, grace depends upon the inability of its subjects. The pathway to salvation starts with recognition of the insufficiency of human ability and leads to the safety of the sufficiency of Jesus.

The following is an acrostic that captures the true essence of saving faith. Take the letters F-A-I-T-H and expand them into this sentence:

FAITH

Forsaking
All
I
Trust
Him

Forsaking all my best efforts—all my claims to goodness, all my strategies to overcome my inadequacies, all available cures to my brokenness, all my attempts at honorable ethics, all my merits and accomplishments, all my religious credentials—I forsake all of that and put my trust in Jesus alone. He alone is the only deserving object of our full trust, and he is the only option that can guarantee our eternal safety.

Someone once wisely observed that sometimes the best way to get out of a hole is to stop digging. That is totally true of the hole of sin because trying to dig out of it only makes it deeper. The best way to get out of the pit of sin is to stop digging. That means putting aside your efforts and looking at an outside source to lift you up and out of the hole you have dug for yourself.

It is intriguing that if a bumblebee is placed in a glass tumbler, even though the bumblebee can fly away, it won't! Instead, the bumblebee burrows around at the bottom of the tumbler looking for a way of escape that does not exist. When all it must do to escape is flap its wings and fly out, the bee will stubbornly persist in its futile efforts to create a way out—until it dies. Why is it that human beings keep burrowing around looking for an escape route that does not exist? All a person must do is to look to Jesus, who will guide that person to exercise their wings of faith, escape the sinful hole they have dug for themselves, and fly heavenward.

It is reasonable to ask that if our good works don't save us, does that mean that once we put our faith in Jesus, we can live any way we want from then on and still be on God's good side? In other words, can I go out and live like hell but still expect to go to Heaven? In our Ephesians 2 passage, in the very next verse it says, "We are his workmanship created in Christ Jesus unto good works." These words clearly imply that one is not saved *by* good works but saved *to do* good works. Here is the best way to state it: good works are not the grounds of one's salvation, just the proof. And so, good works become a validating manifestation of one's saving faith, serving not as the root, but as the fruit, of a person's reconciliation with God.

Here is the best way to state it: good works are not the grounds of one's salvation, just the proof.

Which of the following equations is true—according to most people?

Faith + Good Works = Salvation

Faith = Salvation = Good Works

Which of the following equations is true . . . according to the Bible?

Faith + Good Works = Salvation

Faith = Salvation = Good Works

Most would answer that the first statement is the correct one, but the Bible teaches us the second equation is the correct one. Here is the point to be remembered: a person comes to God out of need, not by way of a showcase of their deeds.

Allow me to conclude with this observation. This question was posed earlier: what is saving faith? This might be the very best way we can state it: saving faith involves coming to the firm conviction that the death of Jesus on the cross in my place for my sins is sufficient for my eternal salvation. Nothing more, nothing less, nothing else. That is it.

At the beginning of this chapter, it was noted that Jesus alone prescribes salvation through self-abandonment, not self-enhancement. All other religions teach that "only you can save you." Christianity teaches: *Only Jesus can save you*. His wise instruction is to look away from oneself to someone else. He has paid the price in full. His perfect sacrifice has satisfied the demands of God's high standard of perfection, the only one that ultimately matters. He has fully atoned for the sins of the world. His death on the cross is alone sufficient for your eternal life. The deal is done! All that's needed is your buy-in.

This chapter has sought to answer two fundamental questions:

What does it mean to be saved?

And,

How is a person saved?

Only when a person's fractured relationship with God has been graciously healed through confident belief in and unwavering reliance upon Jesus, the great physician, whose death on the cross sufficiently secures eternal security, can it be said that a person is saved!

Small Group Interaction

REFLECTION QUESTIONS

- In your words, distinguish between skepticism, ambivalence, and genuine faith?
- Which of the three elements—knowledge, agreement, trust—infuses faith with transformational power? Why?
- Transformational faith in Jesus: what impact would you say such faith might have on your spiritual journey? What relevance does this topic have to your spiritual journey?

Next, Session 5: The Invitation--The Greatest Offer to the Greatest Number of People

FIVE

The Invitation—The Greatest Offer to the Greatest Number of People

In the 1920s, a young man named John Griffith lived in Oklahoma. He was recently married, had a young son named Greg, and dreamed of traveling to "faraway places with strange-sounding names."[24] In the last year of that decade, when the great crash of the American economy and the howling prairie winds turned Oklahoma into a desolate, hopeless, dustbowl state, John packed up his few belongings and headed east with his wife and small son in an old Model A. They made their way to the edge of the Mississippi River, and there he found a job tending to one of the great railroad bridges that spanned the mighty Mississippi. It was his responsibility, day by day, to sit in the control house and open the massive bridge with its huge gears to let the barges and cargo ships go by and then close it again for the trains to roar across the river. He used to sit there, while working, and contemplate where ships were going and what wonderful places they would see.

It was in 1937 that, for the first time, he brought his eight-year-old son, Greg, to work with him. His son was wide-eyed as he watched his father press the lever and saw the huge bridge rise or come down again at his father's will. Surely his father was the greatest man in the world; he controlled this magnificent bridge.

When lunchtime came, he raised the bridge to allow some boats that were scheduled to come by to pass. Then he went with his son over a catwalk to an observation deck that extended fifty feet out over the river. There they could see the boats as they passed. They opened their lunch boxes, and while they ate, he told his son stories about these wonderful places. Time passed. He was telling little Greg about the time the river overflowed with tragic results when, in the middle of the story, he was suddenly startled out of his reverie by the shrieking whistle of a train! He quickly glanced at his watch and saw that it was due in just a couple of minutes.

Griffith didn't panic. He told his son to stay where he was. He leaped to his feet, quickly jumped onto the catwalk, ran back, climbed the steel ladder into the control house, and looked up the river to see that no ships were coming downstream. Then, according to custom, he looked under the bridge to see that there was nothing there.

Then his eyes fell upon a sight that made his heart leap into his throat.

As he looked down into this massive room (the gearbox, it was called), where there were tons of gears that moved this gigantic bridge, there, between the teeth of the two main cogs of the gearbox, was his little son! He had tried to follow his father back and had fallen off the catwalk. He was conscious, but his leg was trapped between the teeth of the gears. If John lowered the bridge, he would most certainly kill his son. What could he do? Immediately, he formed a plan: he would take the rope that was coiled nearby, climb down the ladder, run up the catwalk, tie off that rope, go down, free his son, bring him back up, come back, climb the ladder, throw the lever, and lower the bridge—all before the train arrived. But no sooner had he thought this through than he knew he didn't have near enough time to do all those tasks.

What would he do? His mind panicked; his blood was frozen. What *could* he do? There were four hundred people on that train, which was racing toward the raised bridge. Soon it would come out of the trees at tremendous speed. But this . . . this was his son, his only child! His mother was waiting for her small child at home. Though he was his father, and this was his son, he knew what he had to do.

He buried his head in his left arm and plunged the lever forward. Just as the bridge settled into place, the Memphis Express, with four hundred passengers aboard, came flying out of the trees and roared across the bridge. John Griffith lifted up his tear-streaked face and looked into the windows of the passing train. There was a businessman reading the morning paper and a uniformed conductor looking at his large vest pocket watch. There were ladies sipping coffee in the dining car and a little child was pushing a long spoon into a dish of ice cream. But no one looked at John Griffith, the devastated father. No one looked at the control box. No one looked down into the gear room with its massive gears and the mangled remains of all his hopes and dreams.

He pounded on the glass and shouted, "What's the matter with you people!? Don't you care? Don't you realize that I just sacrificed my son for you? Does this mean anything to you?" No one answered a word, no one bothered to look, no one seemed to care.

The train roared out of sight across the river.

In Jesus' day, a common practice was for men to sacrifice their sons to appease the wrath of their gods for their sins. But the idea that any god would sacrifice his son to satisfy his own wrath toward sinners was inconceivable. However unheard of it may have seemed at that time, that is the central message of the Christian faith, and it is spelled out clearly in one of the more memorable verses in the Bible: "God so loved the world that he gave his only begotten son, that whoever believes in him will not perish but have eternal life" (John 3:16). Assuming that you have absorbed the content of this book in some measure, and that you now understand more deeply what God has done for you, please stop and ask yourself this question: What does this mean to me?

As stated earlier, Christianity is

"The *greatest PERSON*
with the *greatest gift*
of the *greatest benefit*
to the *greatest number* of people
through the *greatest offer.*"

Now attention will be turned to this great offer and to whom it is extended. Most of us have been raised to believe that we should never attend a private event unless we're invited. If we were to go to an invitation-only event or meeting uninvited, that would be seen as rude and inappropriate. One of the most intriguing things about the Christian faith is that it comes with an invitation. And once you are made aware of the invitation, you must decide if you are going to receive it or refuse it. Either way, like any invitation, you can't be neutral about it.

The invitation that Jesus gives is an invitation to a heavenly banquet. It symbolizes entering a love relationship with him. This book was written with the fundamental belief that there is a God who wants a relationship with each of us and will meet us where we are. He invites us into that relationship with words like these: "Come to me, all that are weary and heavy laden, and I will give you rest."

One of the rituals that we observe in the Christian community is communion. On the night he was betrayed, leading to his death, Jesus blessed the bread, broke it, and placed it before his disciples, inviting them to "Take and eat, for this is my body." He then held up a cup, gave thanks for it, and extended it to the disciples with these words, also of invitation: "Take and drink. This is my blood which is to be shed on behalf of many for the forgiveness of sins."

Now, what doesn't lie on the surface of these words is that the language Jesus was using in these statements was the equivalent of a marriage proposal. At this point, further explanation is needed.

Back in Jesus' day, when a groom wanted to propose to his prospective bride, he and his father would journey together to the bride's house, and they would take with them a bottle of wine and a cup. First, they would negotiate a bridal price with the bride and her father, and usually this was quite expensive.

Once that issue was satisfactorily settled, the custom was for the groom's father to pour a cup of wine and hand it to the son. The son would then hold the cup before the prospective bride and say to her, "This is a new covenant which represents my blood being given for you." In effect, he was pledging his life to her and was asking her to pledge hers to him. As for the bride's response, if she took the cup and drank from it, it meant she accepted the marriage proposal and was saying yes. If she took the cup and didn't drink from it but handed it back, that was her way of saying no. It meant she had refused the marriage proposal.

Notice that once a proposal was made, it had to be either accepted or rejected, received or refused. So, when Jesus instituted the Lord's Supper using that same language, he was intentionally issuing a marriage proposal. Jesus says, "This is my body broken for you; take and eat. This is my blood, shed for you; take and drink." These words are an invitation to participate in the heavenly feast, but even more than that, they are a marriage proposal being extended from a heart of sacrificial love. The recipient of the invitation/proposal must either embrace it or turn it down. The Bible is clear that there comes a point at which the proposal, if not acted upon, will be withdrawn. Now that you've participated in an in-depth investigative process of the claims of Christianity, you are in position to make an informed decision on how to respond to the invitation.

Perhaps the most moving depiction of Jesus' sacrificial love for us can be seen in his hanging on the cross with his arms open wide to the world, as if to say, "Come to me."

In conclusion, here is a creative way to respond to Jesus' invitation and let him know what his death means to you. What follows is the script of a letter. I believe that if Jesus were standing before you, he would say something like this:

Dear One,

I lovingly request the honor of your presence at my heavenly banquet table. I created you for a relationship with me. There's an empty place in your heart that can only be filled by my loving presence. I know that you have struggled at times with a sense of unworthiness in your spiritual life, and that at times I seem very distant. However, I came to earth and died for your sins to make it clear I want a genuine and personal relationship with you. If you will put your faith and trust in me, I promise to give you life, abundant and eternal. I'm standing at the door of your heart and knocking. Will you let me in? I want to spend eternity with you. Will you accept my invitation?

Jesus Christ, the Lord

How will you respond?

Dear Jesus,

____

____

____

____

____

____

____

____

____

____

____

____

Your Signature

Date

I want to encourage you to write your response on the blank lines below Jesus' words of invitation. Ask yourself: what is my response to his invitation? What does his brutal death mean to me? If your heart is open to respond to his invitation for the first time, in your own words, express your desire to receive it. If you already know him, then renewing your commitment is probably the thing to do. However, if you are not quite at a point of readiness to respond to the invitation, just express your hesitation on these lines. You may still have unanswered questions or need to do further investigation, and if so, then candidly express your reservations. Either way, I encourage you to write, on the blank lines, thoughts that authentically capture the true intent of your heart at this moment.

PERSONAL STORY: JENNIFER

I grew up in a Christian family. My parents met at a church in East Point when they were 15 and got married at 18, and I think as life progressed and they had kids, you know, they didn't attend church very often. So, for both my brother and I, we were not raised in the church. We knew of Jesus, but we didn't know much about him and what he did for us. We really didn't talk about God, church, or any of that.

Before Jesus was in my life, it's hard to think about what I was doing with my time. I was just kind of "there." I didn't have a lot of friends. I wasn't very outgoing. I wasn't social, you know, participating in anything, and really was just kind of lost.

One day a very close family friend to my mother named Jan was telling us about her new job at The Church of The Apostles where she had begun working as an assistant to one of the pastors. Over time, she would come over on weekends and tell us more about the church. Eventually, she mentioned that the church offered a short course, called Christianity Examined, on how to have a personal relationship with God. She encouraged me to come because she knew something was missing in my life, and though she knew what it was, I didn't. So, she invited me to church when they were having a Guest Sunday, and I attended with her and then enrolled in the course to learn about how one might connect with God.

I had recently visited other churches, and I knew deep down that something was missing from my life. Things were not the way I wanted them to be, so I was ready and willing to learn who Jesus is and what he did for us.

Things were not the way I wanted them to be, so I was ready and willing to learn who Jesus is and what he did for us.

The neat things I liked about the Christianity Examined course were all the evidence, all the history, and how Christianity's roots are based upon historical events. You can't really deny that everything in the Bible is true with all the supporting facts behind it. The comparisons to other religions helped clarify the distinctions between the religions and how they were lacking all the details that Christianity wasn't. I never understood that until I went through the course and learned how evidential and truthful the Christian faith is.

On the last night of Christianity Examined I stood up and walked to the front of the room with everyone else who was seeking to know God. I placed my love letter to Jesus at the foot of the cross, accepting Christ as my Lord and Savior. Jan later told me that she saw a noticeable change in me that night.

At the end of that course, it just felt like it was time to do business with God. I was ready, and he was calling me. In fact, I knew he'd been calling me for a while, but I just never listened and never answered. But on that particular day I did hear his invitation, I responded, and I accepted Christ.

It was hard to make that commitment—to be here week after week—but when I think about it, if I hadn't come forward, I still would be that lost person searching, trying to figure out where I belonged, and looking for what my future holds. By going through Christianity Examined, I was able to learn about Jesus and see how he could positively impact me, and almost immediately things started changing in my life. Now I have a new job, I have great coworkers, and I just became a member of the church, so a lot of things are moving in the right direction for me now.

If I had to describe Jesus to a friend, I would say he can do anything if you just open your heart and let him be a part of your life. Thank you, Jesus!

* * * * *

Final Thoughts

This entire book can be summarized in a single sentence. Christianity is:

Jesus Christ (the *greatest person*)
laid down his life (the *greatest gift*)
to make salvation available (the *greatest benefit*)
to everyone (the *greatest number of people*)
through an open invitation (the *greatest offer*).

Thank you so much for reading this book and allowing your heart and mind to be engaged in the God-question. While significant disagreement exists as to how this question is answered, there is little disagreement as to the significance of the question itself. Nothing has more profound and more far-reaching implications for our lives than how we deal with this issue. Now you must decide: what are you going to do with Jesus' invitation? Jesus gives the world a standing invitation—an invitation that anyone and everyone is always welcome to come to Him.

One final illustration . . .

A pastor waited in line to have his car filled with gas just before a long holiday weekend. The attendant worked quickly, but there were many cars ahead of the pastor. Finally, the attendant motioned the pastor to a vacant pump. "Reverend," said the young man, "I am so sorry about the delay. It seems everyone waits until the last minute to get ready for a long trip."

The minister chuckled. "I know all too well what you mean. It's the same in my line of work."

Please don't wait until the last minute to get ready for your final trip!

One final challenge . . .

My wife and I recently entered a wellness program and have lost 85 pounds between us. After I lost half of the 30 total pounds I ended up losing, my doctor was pleasantly surprised at how much my health indicators had improved. He said, "Why stop now?" Influenced by his encouragement, I kept going and lost another 15 pounds. I am so glad I did because of the quality that additional weight loss has added to my life.

Through reading this book, you have entered a thought process about one of life's most profound questions: belief in God. The first step is to sort what to believe about God, and the next step is to determine why to believe it. The validation of the "what" comes from the "why." This book is very much about the "what," but it's even more about the "why," and hopefully it has elevated, to a new level, your understanding of the way belief in God is designed to work itself out in a person's life. If this book has stimulated your interest in cultivating a more active spiritual life, the question you are likely now facing is the "how."

Our experience has been that interested people who are ready to answer the "how" question need help. Over the last fifteen years we have spent thousands of hours developing growth materials that answer three related questions about Christianity:

What is it?
Why should I believe it?
How do I work it out in my life?

So now, if you have arrived at the "how" question, we strongly encourage you to go to the C128 Ministries website and peruse the resources offered there to help you.

Website: www.c128ministries.org

Now that you have finished this book and are possibly interested in taking a next step toward God, my question for you is, "Why stop now?" I would love to hear your story and would be glad to interact with you further to help shape what your next steps could look like.

Email: drj@c128ministries.org

One final story . . .

PERSONAL TESTIMONY: JAMES SAXON

My name is James Saxon, and I was born in Gadsden, Alabama on November 1, 1951. I have lived in Atlanta since the year 2000, so I am one of many Atlanta transplants. I have been married for the last forty-three years to my wife, Cindy, and we have two daughters, Natalie, who is in her thirties and single, and Adrienne, who is also in her thirties and married with two kids.

First a word about my life before I knew God personally. I grew up in Gadsden, the town I was born in, and lived there until I left to go to college at the age of 18. My father was a salesman, and my mother had a job as the lunchroom manager of the private parochial school I attended through most of junior high school. I graduated from a great high school in 1970, enrolled at the University of Alabama, and graduated as a marketing major four years later. Religion played a key role in my early years. I grew up under the influence of a very devout Catholic mother and a non-practicing Protestant father. I attended Catholic School through the eighth grade and was steeped in this faith. I was an altar boy just as soon as I was old enough to qualify. On a regular basis, I would run to church on weekday mornings to serve 6:30 AM mass, ride to school in a taxi with the nuns, attend the mass at school, and then participate in the morning religion class.

I knew Catholicism cold, and I could recite the entire mass in Latin from memory as a ten-year-old kid. I believed that personal goodness was the way to Heaven. My relationship with God could be described as cordial but distant. In high school, I gradually abandoned my religious foundation and became a ringleader of the wildest hell-raising peer group in my school. My favorite song was "Born to Be Wild" by Steppenwolf, and I enjoyed a reputation as one of the wildest characters in town. I drank like a fish, cursed like a sailor, and was a card-carrying, law-defying citizen. I took the Lord's name in vain at will, and once, while very drunk, rode on the hood of a car that was traveling 85 miles an hour. I was thrown into jail twice for illegal possession of alcohol in my dry county. In college, I was not only disinterested in spiritual things but even cynical toward those who talked with me about a personal relationship with God. My formal, cordial relationship with God had become cold and even hostile in just a few short years.

But that was about to change. At the age of twenty, God intervened and turned my fun, hell-raising world upside down. Halfway through my sophomore year in college, I remember beginning to question my personal values and the way of life I had chosen. As I reflected on my life direction, I admitted to myself that there was a nagging dissatisfaction lurking below the surface in my heart. I began to ponder the spiritual things that my Christian high school friends had shared with me in our previous encounters. I admitted to myself that they had something I didn't.

After four months of personal reflection and many discussions with anyone who was open to talk about it, on the first Monday of June, 1972, I went to see a friend. I had had tense spiritual conflict with this friend in high school, so he was very surprised to see me at his front door. I asked him to explain to me one more time what it meant to be a Christian. He explained that a Christian believed four things: there is a God who created us for his purposes; we have veered away from his purposes for our lives and have lived out our own, creating a destructive distance in our relationship with him; he sent Jesus to remove the barrier of sin between us; and finally, he promises forgiveness, freedom, and abundant life to those who embrace Jesus unconditionally as their Savior and follow him as their Lord. Upon hearing the

I became a Christian and now had a genuine relationship with God that was warm and personal, not cold and formal.

message of salvation for the umpteenth time, I knelt next to the bed in my friend's bedroom and surrendered my life to God on God's terms. I became a Christian and now had a genuine relationship with God that was warm and personal, not cold and formal.

Now that I truly had a genuine, personal faith in God, my life began to dramatically take on a different shape. Within just a few short days, I could no longer take the Lord's name in vain without feeling horribly uncomfortable. I simply could not continue to curse the name of a God who had died for me. Attending church suddenly took on a new dimension, one in which I began to respond joyfully to the presence of God. Within weeks, I began to see women through the eyes of purity. I could now see the person beneath the outward feminine beauty and, for the first time, saw the dignity of the inner person of the opposite gender. Within months I lost interest in drinking and carousing. I realized that I had better things to do with my time.

At the first fraternity chapter meeting that following fall, I actually told my fraternity brothers face to face as a group that I was no longer a member of their hell-raising gang because I now had God in my life. They were as amazed as I was by what had happened to me. I started reading the Bible for the first time in my life and soon realized the Bible was unlike any other book I had ever encountered. I was amazed to discover that I had been raised in a religion that believed in the Bible but had never taught me the Bible. I became so enamored with the Scriptures that a year and a half after I became a Christian, I was memorizing large portions of the Scripture every week.

In regard to the enormous changes God made in my life, a verse in the Bible says it best: "If any man is in Christ, he is a new creature; old things have passed away, behold, things have become new." The transformation in my life was so complete that there was no explanation for it other than as an act of God. It is as if I have lived two vastly different lives, with my relationship with God through Jesus Christ being the dividing line. Today I am a new creature in Christ, more satisfied than ever with the quality my life.

In conclusion, how satisfied are you with your life? If you are less than fulfilled in your life journey, are you open to considering how a more personal relationship with God can make a positive difference? Please consider the strong possibility of a spiritual solution to the emptiness and dissatisfaction in your life. As we now go our separate ways, please keep this in mind: there is a God, he wants a relationship with you, and he will meet you where you are. Thank you for this opportunity to share my spiritual story.

One final request . . . email me (drj@c128ministries.org) and tell me your story!

ENDNOTES

1. Bruce Bickel and Stan Janz, "World Religions and Cults 101," (Eugene, Oregon: Harvest House Publishers, 2002), 21.

2. Baidu Baike, "How did ancient people test the purity of gold? They used a Touchstone," Decent Group (June 15, 2022).

3. D. James Kennedy sermon, "The Incomparable Christ" (Fort Lauderdale – Coral Ridge Ministries), 2.

4. Sanders, *The Incomparable Christ,* (Moody Press, Chicago, IL, 2009), p. 17.

5. Lee Strobel, "Case for Christ" (Grand Rapids, Michigan: Zondervan, 1998), 67.

6. Tim Keller, *The Reason for God* (New York: Riverhead Books, 2008), 87.

7. Tim Keller, *The Reason for God* (New York: Riverhead Books, 2008), 91.

8. Tim Keller, *The Reason for God* (New York: Riverhead Books, 2008), 92.

9. Robert Jastrow, "God and the Astronomers" (New York: W.W. Norton and Company, Inc, 1992), 106-107.

10. Josh McDowell, *Evidence that Demands a Verdict, Volume I* (Campus Crusade for Christ, 1972), p. 73f.

11. Nelson Glueck, *Rivers in the Desert* (New York: Farrar, Strous and Cudahy, 1959), p. 31.

12. D. James Kennedy, "Skeptics Answered" (Sisters, Oregon: Multnomah Books, 1997), p. 41.

13. D. James Kennedy, “Skeptics Answered” (Sisters, Oregon: Multnomah Books, 1997), p. 37.

14. Lee Strobel, “The Case for Christ” (Grand Rapids, Michigan: Zondervan, 1998), p. 199.

15. Peter Stoner, *Science Speaks* (Wheaton, Illinois: Van Kampen Press, 1953), p. 63.

16. D. James Kennedy, “Skeptics Answered” (Sisters, Oregon: Multnomah Books, 1997), p. 51.

17. D. James Kennedy, “Skeptics Answered” (Sisters, Oregon: Multnomah Books, 1997), p. 52.

18. Josh McDowell, *Evidence That Demands a Verdict, Volume I* (Campus Crusade for Christ, 1972), pp. 107-112.

19. Karl Menninger, “Whatever Became of Sin?” (Portland, Oregon: Hawthorn Books, 1973), p. 1.

20. Denis Alexander and Alister McGrath, “Coming to Faith Through Dawkins” (Kregel Publications, Grand Rapids, Michigan, 2023), p. 138.

21. Philip Yancey, *What's so Amazing About Grace,* (Zondervan – 1997), 45.

22. Nicky Gumble, *Alpha--Questions of Life,* (Alpha North America - 2003), 59.

23. Matt Tavares, *Crossing Niagara*, (Candlewick Press – 2016), 24-27.

24. Dennis Hensley, “To Sacrifice a Son,” article cited in a D. James Kennedy sermon.

ADDITIONAL RESOURCES

If you have additional questions, please drop by our website **www.c128ministries.org/** for more information.